Mantras to Hindu Gods & Goddesses

Mantras to Śrī Gaṇeśa, Hanumān, Viṣṇu, Narasiṁha, Gopāla and Garuḍa

Vol. - I

Sri Garib Das Oriental Series No.312

Mantras to Hindu Gods & Goddesses

Mantras to Śrī Gaṇeśa, Hanumān, Viṣṇu,
Narasiṁha, Gopāla and Garuḍa

Vol. - I

Preface

Prof. V.N.Jha
Director,
Centre of Advanced Study in Sanskrit
University of Poona
Pune

Sri Satguru Publications
A Division of
Indian Books Centre
Delhi, India

Published by
Sri Satguru Publications,
Indological and Oriental Publishers
A Division of
Indian Books Centre
40/5, Shakti Nagar,
Delhi-110007
India

(Translations taken from Mantramahohdadhi , Sri Satguru Publications ,
Sri Garib Das Oriental Series 12. 1984)

First Edition : Delhi , 2008

ISBN 81-7030-863-1

Printed by : Sachin Printers, Delhi

Preface

This volume is a collection of *mantras* (spiritual signs) addressed to a number of deities of Indian Spiritual and Religious Culture. These deities are commonly known as gods and goddesses. They are symbols of faith *(śraddhā)* and they take care oı various desires of their devotees and are supposed to satisfy them. Since these gods and goddesses are symbols of *śraddhā* of their devotees, the devotees find a sense of happiness in praising them.

According to the Mīmāṁsakas the deities are of the form of *śabda*. Thus, the devotees identify the gods and goddesses in the form of *śabda* as it could be seen in the *tantra* literature. This seems to be the rationale behind the practice of *mantra*-tradition.

Results are of two type: (i) *dṛṣṭa* (easily verifiable) and (ii) *a-dṛṣṭa* (not easily verifiable). The invocation of a *mantra* leads to the attainment of the results of second category. The recitation of *mantras* remove all hurdle in the path of the fulfillment of the desires of the devotees. The recitaion of *mantras* ward off all *durita-s* (sins or hurdles) by producing *apūrva* intermediate causal link) and ultimately the devotees obtain their desired results.

This volume provides a good collection of *mantras* along with their English translation. It is hoped that the devotees will use these *mantras* as per their symbol of *Śraddhā* with full understanding and devotion to get whatever they want as per their prescribed method of *sādhanā*.

May the gods bless them!

Pune
2006

V.N.Jha
Centre of Advanced Study in Sanskrit
University of Pune

CONTENTS

Preface

Mantras to Śrī Gaṇeśa 1-40

Mantras to Hanumān 41-74

Mantras to Viṣṇu, Narasiṁha,
Gopāla and Garuḍa 75-115

Mantras to Śrī Gaṇeśa

गणेशस्यमनून्वक्ष्येसर्वाभीष्टप्रदायकान् ।
जलं(व)चक्री(क)वह्नि(र) युतःकर्णेंद्वाढ्याचकामिका (तुं) ॥१॥
दारको(ड)दीर्घसंयुक्तो(आ)वायुः(य)कवच(हुं)पश्चिमः ।
षडक्षरोमंत्रराजोभजतामिष्टसिद्धिदः ॥२॥

1-2. I shall mention the Mantras of Gaṇeśa that yield all desired things. Jala means Va then Cakrī with Vahni *i.e.* Kra. The Kāmika with Karṇedu *i.e.* Tum. Then Dāraka with Dirgha *i.e.* Dā, Then Vāyu with Kavala *i.e.* Ya Hum. This is the six syllabled Mantra that will accord all Siddhis to those who resort to it. The Mantra then becomes Vakratuṇḍāya Hum.

भार्गवोमुनिरस्योक्तश्छंदोनुष्टबुदाहृतः ।
विघ्नेशोदेवताबीजंवंशक्तिर्यमितिरितम् ॥३॥

3. The sage of this Mantra is Bhārgava. The metre is Anuṣtup, Vighneṣa is the deity. The Bīja mantra is Vam and the Sakti is mentioned as Yam.

षडक्षरैः सवि धुभिः प्रणवाद्यैर्नमोंतकैः ।
प्रकुर्याज्जातिसंयुक्तैःषडंगविधिमुत्तमम् ॥४॥

4. The excellent rite of Ṣaḍaṅga Nyāsa should be performed severally with the six syllables with Vidhu (Anusvara) at the end and Praṇava in the beginning. Then Namaḥ should be uttered. The Nyāsa should be accompained by the utterances of Svāhā, Vaṣat etc.

भ्रूमध्यकंठहृदयनाभिलिंग पदेषुच ।
मनोर्वर्णान्क्रमान्न्यस्यव्यापय्याथोस्मरेत्प्रभुम् ॥५॥

5. Thereafter the devotee shall perform the Nyāsa in the middle of the eyebrows neck, heart Navel, penis and the feet respectively with the syllables of the Mantra. Thereafter the entire Mantra is used for the Nyāsa all over the body and the Lord is remembered *i.e.* Dhyāna should be performed.

नौका: आदौसकलविघ्ननिवर्तकस्यश्रीगणेशस्यमंत्रान्वक्तुंप्रतिजानीते ॥ गणेशस्येति ॥ मनून्मंत्रान् मन्यंतेसर्वे यैरिति। मंत्रमुद्धरति । जलंव: ॥ चक्रीक: ॥ वह्निर:र: ॥ तेनयुत:तेनयुक्त: ॥ कामिकात् ॥ कर्णेंद्वाढयाउ ॥ बिंदुयुता ॥ तेनतुं ॥ दीर्घआ ॥ तेनयुतोदारकोड: ॥ वायुर्य: ॥ कवचपश्चिमंमतेयस्य- सतथा ॥ वक्रतुंडायहुमितिसविधुभि: सानुस्वारै: ॥ ॐवंनम: हृदयायनम: इत्यादि ॥ व्याप्ययसर्वमंत्रं सर्वशरीरेन्यस्येत्यर्थ: ॥१॥ ॥२॥ ॥३॥ ॥४॥ ॥५॥

Naukā: 1-5. At the outset he cites his intention to explain the Mantras of Gaṇeśa who dispels all obstacles. Manūn means Mantras. Those with which all begin to think. He cites the Mantra with the word Jalam etc.

Jalam means VA

Cakrī means KA

Vahni means RA

Tena Yuta means Joined with that

Kāmikā means TA

Karṇendvāḍhya means having the Bindu and U

Therefore it becomes TUM.

Dīrgha means Ā

Tena Yuta means joined with that

Dāraka means ḌA (therefore ḌĀ)

Yāyu means YA

Kavaca Paścima means having Hum in the end

The whold thing becomes Vakratuṇḍāya Hum

Savidhubhih means along with Anusvāra

Om Namaḥ Hṛdayāya Namaḥ etc. should be used

Vyāpayya means having extended it all over the body by way of Nyāsa

उद्यद्दिनेश्वररुचिंनिजहस्तपद्मैः पाशां कुशाभयवरान्दधतंगजास्यम् ।
रक्तांबरंसकलदुःखहरंगणेशंध्यायेत्प्रसन्नमखिलाभरणाभिरामम् ॥६॥

6. The Dhyāna Verse :–

The Devotee should meditate on Gaṇeṣa who esplendour is like that of the rising sun, who holds the noose and the gesture of fearlessness in the left hands and the boon and the goad in the right hands, whose face resembles that of the elephant, whose clothes are red in colour, who is rendered beautiful by means of all ornaments, who is pleased and who is competent to remove all miseries.

नौका: ध्यानमाह । उद्यादिति ॥ पाशाभयेवामयोः ॥ वरांकुशावन्ययोः ॥६॥

Naukā: 6. He cites Dhyāna by Udyat etc.

Noose and fearlessness in the left hands

Boon and goad in the others.

ऋतुलक्षजपेन्मंत्रमष्टद्रव्यैर्दशांशतः ।
जुहुयान्मंत्रसंसिद्धयैवाडवान्भीजयेच्छुचीन् ॥७॥
इक्षवःसक्त वोरंभाफलानिचिपिटास्तिलाः ।
मोदकानारिकेलानिलाजाद्रव्याष्टकंस्मृतम् ॥८॥

7.8. The mantra has to be repeated six hundred thousand times. The Havan should be performed one tenth of that number (sixty thousand) by means of the eight articles mentioned below. For the purpose of the full realization of the efficacy or the Mantra the devotee shall feed brahmins of pure conduct

The eight articles are Sugarcane, fried wheat flour, bananas, beaten rice, gingelly seeds, sweet meats, coconut and parched grain.

पीठमाधारश क्त्यादिपरतत्त्वांतमर्चयेत् ।
तत्राष्टदिक्षुमध्येचसंपूज्यानवशक्तयः ॥९॥

9. The deities of the pedestal beginning with Ādhāraśakti and ending with Paratattva should be worshipped. The nine Śaktis are to be adored in the eight directions and in the middle.

नौका: वाडवान्विप्रान् ॥७॥

Naukā: 7. Vāḍavān means brahmins.

नौका: द्रव्याष्टकमाह इक्षवइति ॥८॥ ॥९॥

Naukā: 8-9. He mentions the eight articles Ikṣavah etc.

तीव्राचचालिनीनंदाभोगदा कामरूपिणी ।
उग्रातेजोवतीसत्यानवमीविघ्ननाशिनी ॥१०॥

10. The nine Śaktis are Tivrā, Cālini, Nandā, Bhogadā, Kāmarūpiṇi, Ugrā, Tejovati, Satyā and the ninth one Vighna Nāśini.

विनायकस्यमंत्राणामेताःस्युःपीठश क्तयः ।
सर्वशक्तिक्रमांतेतुलासनायहृदंतिकः ॥११॥
पीठमंत्रस्तदीयेनबीजेनादौसमन्वितः ।
प्रदायासनमेतेनमूर्तिंमूलेनकल्पयेत् ॥१२॥
तस्यांगणेशमावाह्यपूजयेदासनादिभिः ।
अश्यर्च्यकुसुमैरीशं कुर्यादावरणार्चनम् ॥१३॥

11-13. The above mentioned are the Śaktis of the pedestal in regard to the Mantras of Vināyaka. The Pithamantra is Sarvaśakti Kamalāsanāya Namaḥ (obeisance to the lotus seat of all the Śaktis). The offering of seat is by means of the Pitha Mantra. Then with the Mūla Mantra the idol is conceived on the pedestal. Gaṇeśa is invoked on that idol. Thereafter the regular Pūjā is proceeded with, not omitting any of the regular features such as offering of flowers, seat etc. Then the worship of the Āvaraṇa is performed.

आग्नेयादिषुकोणेषुहृदयंचशिरः शिखाम् ।
वर्माश्यच्र्याग्रतोनेत्रंदिक्ष्व स्त्रंपूजयेत्सुधीः ॥१४॥

14. Then the intelligent devotee shall worship the six Aṅgas as follows in the corners beginning with South east:—

Gām obeisance to the heart, Gim, Svāhā unto the head, Gūm, Vaṣat unto the tuft and Gaim Hum unto the armour. He then worships Gaum Vauṣat unto the three eyes in the middle and Gaḥ Phat unto the Astra. Thus the Ṣaḍaṅga worship is concluded.

द्वितीयावरणेपूज्याःप्रागाद्यष्टैवशक्तयः ।
विद्यादिमांविद्यात्रीचभोगदाविघ्नघा तिनी ॥१५॥
निधिप्रदीपापापघ्नीपुण्यापश्चाच्छशिप्रभा ।
दलाग्रेषुवक्रतुंडएककदंष्ट्रोमहोदरः ॥१६॥
गजास्यलंबोदरकौविकटोविघ्नराजकः ।
धूम्रवर्णस्तदग्रेषुशक्राद्याआयुधैर्युताः ॥१७॥
एवमावरणैःपूज्यःपंचभिर्गणनायकः ।
पूर्वोक्ताचपुरश्चर्याकार्यामंत्रस्यसिद्धये ॥१८॥

15-18. In the second Āvaraṇa the eight Śaktis are to be worshipped beginning with the east. The Śaktis the Vidyā, Vidhātrī, Bhogadā, Vighnaghātini, Nidhipradipā, Pāpaghni, Puṇyā and Śaśiprabhā. (In the third Āvaraṇa), the following are to be worshipped in the eight petals—*viz.* Vakratuṇḍa, Ekadaṁṣṭra, Mahodara, Gajāsya, Lambodara, Vikaṭa, Vighnarāja and Dhūmravarṇa.

In the fourth and fifth Āvaranas the deities of the quarters Namely Śakra and others, as well as their weapons should be worshipped on the tips of the petals. Thus Goṇanāyaka is to be worshipped with five Āvaraṇas. In order to realize the efficacy of the Mantra the Puraścaraṇa mentioned before has to be performed.

नौका: पीठामंत्रमाह ।। गंसर्वशक्तिकमलासनाय नमः एतनासनंदत्त्वातद्देशे मूलेनमूर्तिकल्पयेत् ।।१०।। ।।१२।। ।।१३।। ।।१४।। ।।१५।। ।।१६।। ।।१७।। ।।१८।।

Naukā: 10-18. He cites the Mantra for the pedestal. The Mantra is Gam Sarvaśaktikamalāsanāya Namaḥ. By this mantra he shall offer seat and in that place he shall conceive the idol with the Mūla Mantra.

ततःसिद्धेमनौ काम्यान्प्रयोगान्साधयेन्निजान् ।
ब्रह्मचर्यरतोमंत्रीजपेद्रविसहस्त्रकम् ।।१९।।
षण्मासमध्याद्दारिद्यंना शयत्येवनिश्चितम् ।
चतुर्थ्यादिचतुर्थ्यंतंजपेद्दशसहस्त्रकम् ।।२०।।
प्रत्यहंजुहुयादष्टोत्तरंशतमतंद्रितः ।
पूर्वोक्तंफलमाप्नोतिषण्मासाद्भक्तितत्परः ।।२१।।

19-21. Afterwords, when the Mantra has been properly mastered, the devotee can proceed with the Kāmya Prayogas (worship for the realization of special desires). The devotee shall strictly adhere to the vow of celibacy for a period of six months'and repeat the Mantra for twelve thousand times. Within the period poverty shall be dispelled completely. Beginning with a Caturthi (4th day in the lunar fortnight) an ending with another he shall repeat the Mantra ten thousand times per day. With perfect concentration he shall perform, Havana one hundred and eight times. The devotee shall surely derive the benefit mentioned before (removal of poverty) within months.

आज्यात्क्तान्नस्यहोमेनभवेद्धनसमृद्धिमान् ।
पृथुकैर्ना रिकेलैर्वामरिचैर्वासहस्त्रकम् ॥२२॥
प्रत्यहंजुह्वतोमासाज्जायतेधनसंचयः ।
जीरसिंधुमरीचाक्तैरष्टद्रव्यैः सहस्त्रकम् ॥२३॥
जुह्वन्प्रतिदिनंपक्षात्स्यात्कुबेरइवार्थवान् ।
चतुःशतं ४४४ चतुश्चत्वारिंशदा ढ्यंदिनेदिने ॥२४॥

22-24. By performing the Havanas with food cooked with ghee he shall flourish in wealth. By performing a thousand Homas every day with the articles, flattened rice, coconut or pepper the devotee shall acquire a great deal of wealth within a month.

The devotee shall perform one thousand Āhutis per day with the eight articles mixed with cummin seed, white borax and pepper. Within a fortnight he shall become wealthy like Kubera.

Every day the devotee shall perform four hundred and forty four Tarpaṇas repeating the Mūla Mantra. Within a Maṇdala (forty nine days) he shall attain whatever he desires.

नौका: प्रयोगानाह ॥ ब्रह्मेति ॥१९॥ ॥२०॥ ॥२१॥ ॥२२॥ ॥२३॥ ॥२४॥

Naukā: 19-24. He mentions the various rites Brahma etc

तर्पयेन्मूलमंत्रेणमंडलादिष्टमाप्नुयात् ।
अथ मंत्रांतरंवक्ष्येसाधकानांनिधिप्रदम् ॥२५॥
रायस्पोषभृगुर्याढ्योददितामेषसात्वतो ।
सदृशौदोरत्नधातुमान्रक्षोगगनंरतिः ॥२६॥
ससद्याबलशार्ङ्गीखंनोषडक्षरसंयुतः ।
एकत्रिंशद्वर्णयुक्तोमंत्रोभीष्टप्रदायकः ॥२७॥

25-27. I shall now mention another Mantra that will accord a treasurd trove to the devotees. This is the thirty one syllabled Mantra which shall accord whatever is desired. The said Mantra is :

"Rāyaspoṣasya Daditā Nidhido Ratnadhātumān Rakṣ ohaṇo Balagahano Vakra Tuṇḍāya Hum".

[The giver of increasing wealth, the giver of treasure trove, the possessor of jewels and metals, the destroyer of evil spirits, extremely strong, Hum unto Vakratuṇḍa].

सायकैस्त्रिभि रष्टाभिश्चतुर्भिःपञ्चभीरसैः ।
मंत्रोत्थितैःक्रमाद्वर्णैःषडंगंसमुदीरितम् ॥२८॥

28-28. The Mantra divided after 5, 3, 8, 4, 5, and 6 letters will constitute the requisite mantras for Ṣaḍaṅga Nyāsa. The sage etc. and the procedure for adoration etc. are as before. This mantra is the bestower of treasure trove.

नौकाः मंडलादेकोनपंचाशद्दिमध्येइष्टंप्राप्नुयात् ॥२५॥

मंत्रांतरमाह ॥ रायस्पोषेति स्वरूपं भृगुःसः ॥ याढथोयकार युतः ॥ मेषोन् ॥ सात्वतोधू ॥ तौसदृशौइयुतौ ॥ गगनंहः रतिर्णः ॥ ससद्याऊँयुताः ॥ शार्ङ्गीगः ॥ खंहः ॥ अन्यत्स्वरूपम् ॥ षडक्षरः पूर्वोक्तः यथा रायस्पोषस्य-ददितानिधिदोरत्नधातुमान्रक्षोह्णोबलगह नोवक्रतुंडायहुमित्येकत्रिंशद्वर्णः ॥२६॥ ॥२७॥ ॥२८॥

Naukā: 25-28. Maṇḍalāt means within 49 days Sadṛśau means. joined with I. Gaganam means Ha. Rati means Ṅa. Sasadyāh means having Om Śārṅgī means Ga. Kham means Ha. The other things are the real forms Ṣaḍakṣara is what is mentioned before. Therefore the whole Mantra of thirty one syllables is – "Rāyaspoṣasya Daditā Nidhido Ratna Dhātumān Rakṣohaṇo Bala Gahano Vakratuṇḍāya Hum".

ऋष्याद्यर्चाप्रयोगाः स्युःपूर्ववन्निधिदोह्ययम् ।
पद्मनाभयुतोभानुर्मेधासद्यसमन्विता ॥२९॥
लकावनंतमारूढौवायुः पावकमोहिनी ।
षडक्षरोयमादिष्टोभजतामिष्टदोमनुः ॥३०॥

29-30. The six syllabled Mantra is mentioned as Medholkāya Svāhā (Svāhā unto the fiery flame of intellect). It is ordained that this mantra is the bestower of the desires of those who resort to it. Everything regarding the adoration is as before.

नौका: पूर्ववत्षड्वर्णवत् ॥२९॥

मंत्रांतरमाह ॥ पद्मेति ॥ भानुर्मः पद्मनाभए ॥ तद्युतःमे । धाधः ॥ सद्यओं३म् ॥ तद्युतालकौलकारककारौ ॥ अनंतमाकारमारूढौ ॥ वायुर्यः ॥ पावकगेहिनीस्वाहा ॥ मेघोल्कायस्वाहेतिषड्वर्णः ॥३०॥

Naukā: 29-30. Pūrvavat means as mentioned in the case of six syllabled mantra.

He mentions another Mantra Padma etc. Bhānu means Ma. Padmanabha means E joined to that it becomes Me Medhā means Gha Sadya – or Lakau joined with that means the letters La and Ka Ananta means the letter Ā therefore, it becomes Lkā Vāyu means Ya. Pāvaka Gehinī means Svāhā. Therefore the six syllabled Mantra is Megholkāya Svāhā.

पूर्ववत्सर्वमेतस्यसमाराधनमीरितम् ।
लकुलीदृशमारूढौभृगुतौलोहितःसदृक् ॥३१॥

वकःसदीर्घश्चःसाक्षिर्लिखेन्मंत्रःशिरोंतिमः ।
नवाक्षरोमनुश्चास्यकंकोलः परिकीर्तितः ॥३२॥
विराट्छंदोदेवतातुस्याद्वैचोच्छिष्टनायकः ।
द्वाश्यांत्रिभिर्द्वयेनाथद्वाश्यांसकलमंत्रतः ॥३३॥

31-33. The nine syllabled Mantra is formed like this:–

Hasti Piśāci Likhe Svāhā.

The Sage of this Mantra is Kaṁkola, the metre is Virāṭ and the deity is Ucchiṣṭagaṇapati. The Pañcāṅga Nyāsa is with the letters divided like 2,3,2,2 and the whole Mantra.

नौकाः मंत्रांतरमाह ॥ लकुलीति ॥ लकुलीहकारः ॥ भृगुतौसकारत-कारौदृशमारूढौइकारयुतौ तेनस्ति । लोहितःपःसदृक् इयुतः ॥ वकः शः ॥ सदीर्घःआयुतः ॥ चस्वरूपम् ॥ साक्षीइयुतः ॥ लिखेस्वरूपंशिरोंतिकस्वाहांतः ॥ हस्तिपिशाचिलिख स्वाहेतिनवार्णः ॥३१॥ ॥३२॥

नौकाः पञ्चांगमाह ॥ द्वाम्यामिति ॥ हरितहृदयायनमइत्यादि ॥३३॥

Naukā: 31-32. He cites another Mantra Lakulī etc. Lakulī means letter Ha. Bhṛgutau means letters SA and TA. Dṛśamārūḍhau means joined with I. Therefore it becomes Sti. Lohita means Pa. Sadṛk means joined with I. Vaka means Śa. Sadīrgha means having Ā. Ca is the form itself Sākṣī means having I. Likhe is the form itself. Śirontika means ending with Svāhā. Hence the nine syllabled Mantra is Hastipiśācilikhe Svāhā.

Naukā: 33. He mentions Pañcāṅganyāsa with the word Dvābhyām. Hence Hasti obeisance to the heart etc. should be used.

पंचां गान्यस्यकुर्वीतध्यायेत्तंशशिशेखरम् ।
चतुर्भुजंरक्ततनुंत्रिनेत्रंपाशांकुशौमोदकपात्रदंतौ ।
करैर्दधानं सरसीरुहस्थमुन्मत्तमुच्छिष्टगणेशमीढे ॥३४॥

34. For this Mantra the Nyāsa is only in five Aṅgas. The Moon-crested lord is to be meditated upon.

Dhyāna Verse : I meditated upon Ucchiṣṭagaṇapati who has four hands and three eyes whose body is red, who holds the goad and the Vessel of sweet meats in the right hands and the noose and the task in the left hands, who is seated in the lotus and who is Unmatta (highly elated and mad).

लक्षमेकंजपेन्मंत्रंदशांशंजुहुयात्तिलैः ।
पूर्वोक्तेपूजये त्पीठेविधिनोच्छिष्टविघ्नपम् ॥३५॥
आदावंगानिसंपूज्याब्रह्माद्यान्दिक्षपूजयेत् ।
ब्राह्मीमाहेश्वरी चैवकौमारीवैष्णवीपरा ॥३६॥
वाराहीचतर्थेद्राणीचामुंडारमयासह ।
ककुप्सुवक्रतुंडाद्यान्दश सुप्रतिपूजयेत् ॥३७॥
वक्रतुंडैककदंष्ट्रौचतथालंबोदराभिधः ।
विकटोधूम्रवर्णश्चविघ्नश्चापिगजाननः ॥३८॥
विनायकोगणपतिर्हस्तिदंताभिधोंतिमः ।
इंद्राद्यानपिवज्राद्यान्पूजयेदावृतिद्वये ॥३९॥

35-39. The Japa of this Mantra is 100,000 times and the Havana with gingelly seeds is for ten thousand times. The devotee shall duly worship Ucchiṣṭagaṇapati in the pedestal as before. At the outset the ancillaries are to be worshipped. Then the Mothers Brāhmi etc. are to be worshipped in the eight directions. They are Brāhmī, Māheśvarī, Kaumārī, Vaiṣṇavī, Vārāhī, Indrāṇī, Cāmuṇḍā and Ramā (*i.e.* Lakṣmi).

Then the devotee shall worship Vakratuṇḍa etc. in the ten directions :–

They are Vakratuṇḍa, Ekadaṁṣṭa, Lambodara, Vikaṭa,

Dhūmṛavaṇa, Vighna, Gajānana, Vināyaka, Gaṇapati and Hastidanta the last one.

In the next two Āvaraṇas he shall adore Indra and others as well as Vajra and other weapons.

After realising the Mantra thus the devotee shall perform the rites for the achievement of the desired objectives.

नौकाः ध्यानमाह ।। चतुर्भुजमिति ।। अंकुशमोदकपात्रेद क्षयोः अन्ययोरन्ये ।।३४।। ।।३५।। ।।३६।। ।।३७।। ।।३८।। ।।३९।।

Naukā: 34-39. He cites the Dhyāna by Caturbhujam etc. In the right hands goad and Vessel of Sweetmeat. The other two in the other hands.

एवंसिद्धेमनौमंत्रीप्रयोगान्कर्तुमर्हति ।
स्वांगुष्ठप्रतिमांकृत्वाकपिनासितभानुना ।।४०।।
गणेशप्रतिमां रम्यामुक्तलक्षणलक्षिताम् ।
प्रतिष्ठाप्यविधानेनमधुनास्नापयेच्च्यताम् ।।४१।।

40-41. The idol of Gaṇeśa should be made either of red Sandal wood or white Arka tree and shall be of the size of the thumb of the devotee. It shall be beautiful and having all the characteristics as mentioned before [in the Dhyāna Verse (34)] After due installation it shall be bathed in honey.

आरश्यद कृष्णभूतादियावच्छुक्लाचतुर्दशी ।
सगुडंपायसंतस्मैनिवेद्यप्रजपेन्मनुम् ।।४२।।
सहस्त्रंप्रत्यहंतावज्जुहु यात्सघृतैस्तिलैः ।
गणेशोहमितिध्यायन्नुच्छिष्टेनावृतोरहः ।।४३।।
पक्षाद्राज्यमवाप्नोति नृपजोन्यो पिवानरः ।

42-43½. Starting with the fourteenth day in the dark half and ending with the fourteenth day of the bright half.

Milk pudding with treacle should be offered as Naivedya and the Mantra should be repeated. Gingelly seeds mixed with ghee should be used for Havana and everyday it is performed a thousand time. The devotee shall do this in a secluded spot with the meditation "I am Gaṇeśa". He shall not wash the mouth after taking food. He shall also be neaked. Whether he is born in a royal family or not, the devotee shall gain a kingdom within a fortnight.

नौका: प्रयोगानाह ।। स्वेति ।। कपिनारक्तचंदनेन ।। सितभानुनाश्वेतार्कर्णवाप्रतिमाकार्य्या ।।४०।। ।।४१।। ।।४२।।

नौका: अनावृतोनिर्वस्त्र: ।।४३।।

Naukā: 40-42. He cites procedures saying Sva etc. Kapinā means with red sandal. Sitabhānunā means by white Arka. The idol can be made with either.

Naukā: 43. Anāvṛta means Having no cloth.

कुलालमृत्स्नाप्रतिमापूजितैवंसुराज्यदा ।।४४।।
वल्मीकमृत्कृतालाभमेवमिष्टान्प्रयच्छति ।
गौडीसौभाग्यदासैवंलावणीक्षोभयेदरीन् ।।४५।।

44-45. The adoration of an idol made of potter's mud (clay) shall bestow a good kingdom. The idol made of the mud derived from ant-hill, when adored, shall bestow profits and everything desired. The idol made of molasses and treacle bestows all fortunes. The idol made of salt shall make the enemies agitated.

निंबजानाशयेच्छत्रून्प्रतिमैवंसमर्चिता ।
मध्वक्तैर्हो मतोलाजैर्वशयेदखिलंजगत् ।।४६।।

46. The idol made of Margosa tree and worshipped thus shall destroy enemies. Fried grain smeared with honey should be used for Homa. The devotee shall then captivate and keep under control the entire universe.

नौकाः वल्मीकमृत्तिकाप्रतिमैवंपूजितालाभदेति ।।४५।। ।।४६।।

Naukā: 45-46. The idol made of Ant-hill clay thus brings fortune.

सुप्तोधिशय्यसुच्छिष्टोजपञ्छत्रून्वशंनयेत् ।

कटुतैलान्वितै राजीपुष्पैर्विद्वेषयेदरीन् ।।४७।।

47. Lying down on the bed and remaining Ucchiṣta (*i.e.* not washing the mouth after eating) the devotee shall repeat the Mantra. He can make enemies come under his sway. If the Homa is performed with the flowers of black mustard smeared with mustard oil the devotee shall alienate the enemies.

नौकाः अधिशय्यंशय्यायाम् ।। कटुतैलंसर्षपतैलम् ।।४७।।

Naukā: 47. Adhiśayyam means on the bed.

Kaṭutailam means Mustrad oil.

द्यूतेविवादेसमरेजप्तोयंजयमावहेत् ।

कुबेरोस्यमनोर्जापान्निधीनां स्वामितामयात् ।।४८।।

48. While playing at the game of dice, or arguing or fighting, the Mantra can be repeated and thereby the devotee shall surely win. Kubera repeated this Mantra and became the possessor of treasure troves.

लेभातेराज्यमनरिवानरेशबिभीषणौ ।

रक्तवस्त्रांगरागाढ्यस्तांबूलंनिश्यद ञ्जपेत् ।।४९।।

यद्वानिवेदितंतस्मैमोदकंभक्षयञ्जपेत् ।

पिशितंवाफलंवापितेनतेनबलिंहरेत् ।।५०।।

49-50. The lord of the the monkeys (Sugriva) and Vibhīṣaṇa acquired kingdom without enemies.

The devotee shall wear red cloth, or apply red, unguents. He shall chew betel in the night and while chewing it repeat the Mantra. He shall offer as oblation meat or fruit along with betel leaves. The devotee can repeat the Mantra while eating the sweet-meat offered previously as Naivedya to the lord.

नौका: अनरिशत्रुहीनम् ॥४९॥

नौका: तेनताम्बूलादिना ॥५०॥

Naukā: 49. Anari means free of enemies.

Naukā: 50. Tena refers to with betel leaf etc.

सेंदुःस्मृतिस्तथाकाशंमन्विंवद्वाढ्यौचसृष्टिलौ ।

पंचांतकशिवौतद्वदुच्छिष्टगभगान्वितः ॥५१॥

उमा कांतःश्यायमांतेहायक्षायासबिंदुयः ।

बलिरित्येषकथितोनवेंद्वर्णोबलेर्मनुः ॥५२॥

51-52. The Mantra for the oblation is of nineteen Syllables :–

"Gam Ham Klaum Glaum Ucchiṣṭa Gaṇeśāya Mahā Yakṣāyāyam Baliḥ". (This oblation is for the great Yakṣa Gaṇeśa in the form of Ucchiṣṭa).

नौका: बलिमंत्रमाह ॥ स्मृतिर्गः ॥ सेन्दुस्सानुस्वारः ॥ आकाशंहः ॥ तथासानुस्वारः । सृष्टिलौककारलकारौ ॥ कीदृशौ मन्विं द्वाढ्यौ- औकारानुस्वारयुतौ। तेनक्लौं ॥ पंचांतकशिवौगकारलकारौतद्वन्मन्विद्राढ्यौंग्लौं ॥ उच्छिष्टगस्वरूपम् ॥ भगा न्वितःउमाकांतः ॥ एकारयुतोणःणे ॥ सबिंदुर्यःसानुस्वारोयकारः ॥ अन्यत्स्वरूपम् ॥ मन्त्रोयथा ॥ गंहंक्लौंग्लौंउच्छिष्ट गणेशायमहायक्षायायंबलिः इत्येकोनविंशत्यर्णोबलिमंत्रः ॥५१॥ ॥५२॥

Naukā: 51-52. He cites the Mantra for oblation Smṛti means Ga. Sendu means along with Anusvāra. Ākāśa means Ha. It is also with Anusvāra. Sṛṣṭilau means letters Ka and La How ? Manuindvāḍhyau means having Au and Anusvāra. Therefore, it becomes Klaum. Pañcāntaka Śivau means letters Ga and La Tadvat means like that viz. with Au and Anusvāra Ucchiṣṭaga is the form itself Bhagānvita Umā Kānta means Ṅa with E i.e. Ṅe. Sabindu Ya means Yam. The other things refers to the form itself. Then the Mantra becomes "Gam Ham Klau Glau Ucchiṣṭagaṇeśāya Mahā Yakṣāyāyam Baliḥ".

ध्रुवोमायासेंदुशा ङ्गिर्बीजाढ्योनववर्णकः ।
द्वादशार्णोमनुः प्रोक्तःसर्वमस्यनवार्णवत् ॥५३॥
ताराद्यश्चगणेशाद्योनवा र्णोदशवर्णकः ।
द्विविधोस्योपासनंतुप्रोक्तमन्यन्नवार्णवत् ॥५४॥
ध्रुवोहृदुच्छिष्टगणेशायतेतुनवाक्षरः ॥
एकोनविंशत्पर्णाढ्योमनुर्मुन्यादिपूर्ववत् ॥५५॥
त्रिभिःसप्त भिरक्षिश्यांत्रिभिर्द्वाश्यांद्वयेनच ।
मंत्रोत्थितःसुधीर्वर्णैःकुर्यादंगंपुरार्चनम् ॥५६॥

53-54. The nine syllabled Mantra mentioned before can be made into twelve syllabled Mantra by adding Om Hrīm and Gam in the beginning. Everthing such as Nyāsa, Dhyāna etc. is the same as in the case of the nine syllabled Mantra.

The nine syllabled Mantra can be converted into ten syllabled Mantra by adding (Tāra) Om or (Gaṇeśa) Gam in the beginning.

55-56. Now the nineteen syllabled Mantra is being mentioned. Namely "Om Nama Ucchiṣṭa Gaṇeśāya Hasti Piśāci Likhe Svāhā". The Ṣadaṅga Nyāsa is to be performed by dividing the syllables of the Mantra at 3, 7, 2, 3, 2 and 2 in the same way the Aṅga adoration sage etc. as before.

नौकाः मंत्रांतरमाह ॥ ध्रुव इति ॥ ध्रुव ओं ।

मायाह्रीं । शार्ङ्गिगःसेंदुःअनुस्वारसहितः ॥ गंत्रिबीजाढयः ॥ स्पष्टम् । यथा ओं ह्रींगंहस्तिपिशाचिलिखेस्वाहेतिद्वादशार्णः ॥५३॥

नौका: ताराद्योयथा ।। ओं हस्तिपिशाचिलिखेस्वाहा ।। गणेशाद्योयथा ।। गंहस्तिपिशाचिलिखेस्वाहा ।।५४।।

नौका: मन्त्रान्तरमाह ।। ध्रुवेति ।। ध्रुव:प्रणव: हृन्नम: स्वरूपमन्यत् ।। मन्त्र:।। ओंनमउच्छिष्टगणेशायहस्तिपिशाचिलिखे स्वाहा इत्येकोनविंशतिवर्ण: ।। मुन्यादीति ।। ऋषिश्छंदोदेवता नवार्णवत् ।।५५।।

नौका: षडंगमाह ।। त्रिभिरिति ।। अर्च्चनंपुरापूर्ववदित्यर्थ: ।।५६।।

Naukā: 53. He cites another Mantra Dhruva etc. Dhruva means Om. Māyā means Hrīm. Śārṅgī means Ga. Sendu means having Anusvāra. Ga Tribījaḍhya. Hence the Mantra is Om Hrīm Gam Hastipiśāci Likhe Svāhā becomes twelve syllabled Mantra.

Naukā: 54. That beginning with Tāra is Om Hasti Piśāci Likhe Svāhā. That beginning with Gaṇeśa is Gam Hastipiśāci Likhe Svāhā.

Naukā: 55. He cites another Mantra Dhruva etc. Dhruva means Praṇava. Hṛt means Namaḥ. Hence Mantra is "Om Nama Ucchiṣṭa Ganeśāya Hasti Piśaci Likhe Svāha" nineteen syllables. The sage etc. as in the case of the nine syllabled Mantra.

Naukā: 56. He cites Ṣadanga Nyāsa with Tribhiḥ etc. Purā means as before.

तारोनमोभगवते झिंटीशश्चतुराननः ।
दंष्ट्रायहस्तिमुच्चार्यखायलंबोदरायच ।।५७।।
उच्छिष्टमवियद्दीर्घात्मनेपाशों कुशःपरा ।।
सेंदुःशार्ङ्गीभगयुतेद्वेमेधेवह्निकामिनी ।।५८।।
उच्छिष्टगणनाथस्यमनुरद्रिगुणाक्षरः ।
गणकोमुनिराख्यातोगायत्रीच्छन्दईरितः ।।५९।।
उच्छिष्टगणपोदेवोजपेदुच्छिष्टएवतम् ।
सप्तदिग्बाणसप्ताब्धियुगार्णैरङ्गकंमनोः ।।६०।।

57-60. Now the Mantra of Thirty seven syllables of Ucchiṣṭa Gaṇanātha is being mentioned *viz.*

"Om Namo Bhagavate Ekadaṁṣṭrāya Hastimukhāya Lambodarāya Ucchiṣṭamahātmane Ām Krom Hrīm Gam Ghe Ghe Svāhā" (Oṁ obeisance unto lord Lambodara, Ucchiṣṭa Mahātman having the face of an elephant and one tusk).

The sage is said to be Gaṇaka.

The metre is Gāyatrī.

The deity is Ucchiṣṭagaṇapa.

The devotee shall remain Ucchiṣṭa while repeating the Mantra. The Ṣaḍaṅga Nyāsa and the adoration is with syllables divided respectively 7, 10, 5, 7, 4 and 4.

The Dhyāna Verse for meditation. I seek refuge in Ucchiṣṭagaṇapati the son of Ambā (Goddess Pārvati) who is seated in the lotus, who holds bow and noose in the left hands and arrows and goad in the right hands and who is (eager to be) engaged in sexual intercourse with his naked wife.

नौका: मंत्रांतरमाह ।। तारइति ।। झिंटीश: ए ।। चतुराननः कः ।। दीर्धवियत् हा ।। पाशआं ।। अंकुशःक्रा पराह्रीं ।। सेन्दुशार्ङ्गीगं ।। भगयुतेद्वेमेधे ।। एकारयुतघद्वयम् ।। वह्निकामिनीस्वाहा ।। अन्यत्स्व रूपम् ।। ओं३म् नमोभगवतेएकदंष्ट्रायहस्तिमुखायलम्बोदरायउच्छिष्टमहात्मनेआंक्रोंह्रींगघेघेस्वाहा ।। अद्रिगुणाक्षरः सप्तत्रिं शदक्षरः ।।५७।। ।।५८।। ।।५९।।

नौका: षंडगमाह ।। सप्तेति ।।६०।।

Naukā: 57-59. He cites another Mantra Jhiṇṭīśa means E. Caturānana means Ka. Dīrghaviyat means Hā. Pāśa=Ām, Aṇkuśa=Krom, Parā=Hrīm, Sendu Śārṅgi=Gam Bhagayute Dve Medhe means two Ghe's. Vahni Kāmini means Svāhā. The other thing the form itself.

Therefore the Mantra becomes :–

"Om Namo Bhagavate Ekadaṁṣṭrāya Hastimukhāya Laṁbodarāya Ucchiṣṭamahātmane Ām Krom Hrīm Gam Ghe Ghe Svāha". Adriguṇākṣara means 37 syllabled Mantra.

Naukā: 60. He says Ṣaḍaṅga Nyāsa with the word Sapta.

शरान्धनुः पाशसृणीस्वहस्तैर्दधानमारक्तसरोरुहस्थम् ।
विवस्त्रमत्यांसुरतप्रवृत्तमुच्छिष्टमम्बासुतमाश्रयेहम् ॥६१॥
लंक्षजपेद्धृतैर्हुत्वातद्दशांशप्रपूजयेत् ।
पूर्वोक्तपीठेस्वाभीष्टसिद्धयेपूर्ववद्विभुम् ॥६२॥

62. For the sake of attaining the desired benefits the devotee shall repeat the Mantra a hundred thousand times and after performing Homa with ghee ten thousand times with all the requisite adoration of the pedestal proceed ahead with the worship of the lord.

नौकाः ध्यानमाह ॥ शरानिति ॥ धनु:पाशौवामयोः ॥ शरांकुशौदक्षयोः ॥६१॥ ॥६२॥

Naukā: 61-62. Dhyāna is cited in the Verse. Bow and noose in the left hands. Arrow and goad in the right hands.

कृष्णाष्टम्यादितद्भूतंयावत्ताञ्जपेन्मनुम् ।
प्रत्यहंसाष्टसाहस्त्रंजुहुयात्तद्दशांशतः ॥६३॥
तर्पयेदपिमं त्रोयंसिद्धिमेवंप्रयच्छति ।
धनंधान्यंसुतान्पौत्रान्सौभाग्यमतुलंयशः ॥६४॥

63-64. Beginning with the eighth day of the dark lunar half and ending with the same fourteenth day the devotee shall repeat the Mantra eight thousand five hundred times per day and perform Homas eight hundred and fifty times. He shall also perform Tarpaṇa. Thus the Mantra will accord due benefits such as wealth, grain, sons, grandsons all good fortune and unparalleled reputation.

मूर्तिंकुर्य्याद्ग णेशस्यशु भ्राहेनिम्बदारुणा ।
प्राणप्रतिष्ठांकृत्वाथतदग्रेमंत्रमाजपेत् ॥६५॥

यंध्यात्वादासवत्सोपिवश्योभवति निश्चितम् ।
नदीजलंसमादायसप्तविंशतिसंख्यया ॥६६॥
मंत्रयित्वामुखंतेनप्रक्षाल्येशसभांव्रजेत् ।
पश्येद्यंदृश्यतेयेनसवश्योजायतेक्षणात् ॥६७॥

65-67. The devotee shall make the idol of the lord with the neem tree (Margosa) on an auspicious day. He shall then perform the prāṇa pratiṣthā (Installation of Vital airs) and repeat the Mantra in front of it. The deity, meditating on whom the devotee repeats Mantra, becomes under his control like a slave.

The devotee brings water from the river and invokes it with Mantra twenty seven times. He then washes his faces thereby and goes to the Court of the king. The person whom he sees and the person by whom he is seen comes under his control in an instant.

चतुःसहस्त्रंधत्तूरपुष्पाणिमनुनार्पयेत् ।
गणेशायनृपा दीनांजनानांवश्यताकृते ॥६८॥

68. For the sake of getting people like kings and others under one's control one shall adore Gaṇeśa with four thousand Dhattura flowers repeating the Mantra.

सुंदरीवामपादस्यरेणुमादायतत्रतु ।
संस्थाप्यगणनाथस्यप्रतिमां प्रजपेन्मनुम् ॥६९॥
तांध्यात्वारविसाहस्त्रंसासमायातिदूरतः ।
श्वेतार्केणाथनिम्बेनकृत्वामूर्तिंधृतासुकाम् ॥७०॥
चतुर्थ्यां पूजयेद्रात्रौरक्तैःकुसुमचंदनैः ।
जप्त्वासहस्त्रंतांमूर्तिंक्षिपेद्रात्रौसरित्तटे ॥७१॥
स्वेष्टंकार्य्यंसमाचष्टेस्वप्ने तस्यगणाधिपः ।
सहस्त्रंनिम्बकाष्ठानांहोमादुच्चाटयेदरीन् ॥७२॥

69-72. The devotee shall take the dust from the left foot of a beautiful woman and place the idol of Gaṇeśa therein and repeat the Mantra twelve thousand times all the while meditating on her. She will come to him even if she goes far off.

The devotee makes the idol of the lord with white Arka tree or Nimba (Margosa) and then performs Prāṇapratiṣṭhā. He then worships it with red flowers and sandal paste on the night of the fourth day. After repeating the Mantra a thousand times he flings the idol on the bank of the river during the night. Lord Gaṇeśa shall come to him in dreams and tell him about the desired objective.

By performing Homa with a thousand Margosa twigs the devotee can drive away his enemies.

नौका: तद्भूतंयावत्कृष्णचतुर्दशीपर्य्यन्तम् ।।६३।। ।।६४।। ।।६५।। ।।६६।। ।।६७।। ।।६८।। ।।६९।।

नौका: धृतासुकां कृतप्राणप्रतिष्ठाम् ।।७०।। ।।७१।। ।।७२।।

Naukā: 63-69. Tadbhūtam Yāvat means till the fourteenth day of the dark half.

Naukā: 70-72. Dhṛtāsukām means where the rite of Prāṇa Pratiśṭhā has been performed.

वज्रिणःसमिधांहोमाद्रिपुर्य्यमपुरंव्रजेत् ।
वानरस्यास्थिसंजप्तंक्षितमुच्चाटयेद्गृहे ।।७३।।

73. If Homa is performed by the twigs of Vajrī plant (Snuhi-Milk hedge plant) the enemy will go the abode of Yama (*i.e.* die). If the bone of a monkey is invoked with Mantra and thrown at a house it can do the Uccaṭana (Driving away).

जप्तंनरास्थिकन्यायागृहेक्षिप्तंतदाप्तिकृत् ।
कुलालस्यमृदा स्त्रीणांवामपादस्यरेणुना ।।७४।।

कृत्वापुत्तलिकांतस्याहृदिस्त्रीनामसंलिखेत् ।
निखनेन्मंत्रसंजप्तैर्निम्बकाष्ठः क्षिताविमाम् ॥७५॥
सोन्मत्ताभवतिक्षिप्रमुद्धृतायांसुखं भवेत् ।
शत्रोरेवंकृतासातुलशुनेनसमन्विता ॥७६॥
शरावान्तर्गतासम्यक्पूजिता द्वारिविद्विषः ।
निखातापक्षमात्रेणशत्रूच्चाटनकृत्स्मृता ॥७७॥

74-77. If the human bone is invoked with Mantra and thrown into the house of a girl it can help the devotee in getting her.

The devotee makes an idol with the potter's clay as well as the dust from the left feet of woman. He then writes the name of a woman in the heart of the idol. He then invokes Margosa twigs with the Mantra and buries the idol along with the Margosa twigs into the ground. The women immediately becomes mad. If the twigs and the idol are taken out she will become well again.

The same procedure can be adopted in the case of an enemy. His form should be made and the rite should be performed as before with Laśuna (garlic). As a result of this the enemy becomes mad.

The idol (of the lord) shall be kept in a platter, adored well and buried under the ground at the portals of the enemy. It shall drive away the enemy within a fortnight.

नौकाः वज्रीस्नुही ॥७३॥ ॥७४॥ ॥७५॥ ॥७६॥ ॥७७॥

Naukā: 73-77. Vajrī means Snuhī.

विषमेसमनुप्राप्तोसितार्कारिष्टदारुजम् ।
गणपं पूजितंसम्यक्कुसुमैरक्तचन्दनैः ॥७८॥
मद्यभाण्डस्थि
तंहस्तमात्रेतंनिखनेत्स्थले ।
तत्रोपविश्य प्रजपेन्मंत्रीनक्तंदिवामनुम् ॥७९॥

सप्ताहमध्येनश्यंतिसर्वेघोराउपद्रवाः ।
शत्रवोवशमायान्तिवर्द्धन्तेधनसंपदः ॥८०॥

78-80. If one is faced with difficult circumstances one shall resort to this rite :–

The devotee makes an idol of Gaṇeśa with white Arka or Margosa tree and adores it well with red flowers and red sandal. He then places it on a liquor pot and buries both one hand deep into the ground. He then sits on the ground above and repeats the Mantra day and night. Within a week all his difficulties shall be removed. All the enemies come under his control and all the wealth and assets increase.

नौकाः अरिष्टोनिंबः ॥७८॥ ॥७९॥

Naukā: 78-79. Ariṣta means Nimba (Margosa).

दुष्टस्त्रीवामपाद स्यरजसानिजदेहजैः ।
मलैर्मूत्रपुरीषाद्यैः कुम्भकारमृदापिच ॥८१॥
एतःकृत्वागणेशस्यप्रति मांमद्यभांडगाम्
संपूज्यनिखनेद्भूमौहस्तार्द्धेपूरितेपुनः ॥८२॥
संस्थाप्यवह्निंजुहुयात्कुसुमैर्हयमा रजैः ।
सहस्त्रंसाभवेद्दासीतन्वाचमनसाधनैः ॥८३॥
एवमादिप्रयोगांस्तुनवार्णेनापिसाधेयत् ।

81-83½. If the devotee wants to exert effective control over a wicked worman he shall perform the following rite:–

He collects the dust from her left foot and then mixes it with his own urine faces and other bodily dirts as well as potter's clay making an idol thereof. The idol is placed in a liquor pot and worshipped duly the entire thing is buried into the ground to the depth of half a hand (23 cms) and covered well. Fire is kindled above and a thousand Āhutis are performed with Karavīra flowers. That wicked women becomes his slave.

These and other rites can be performed wih the nine syllabled Mantra also with reduced Ācamana and other ancillaries.

नौका: हयमारज: करवीरोत्थै: ॥८३॥

Naukā: 83. Hayamārajaiḥ means with those of Karavīra.

तारोह न्तिमुखायाथङेन्तोलम्बोदरस्तथा ॥८४॥
उच्छिष्टान्तेमहात्माङेपाशाङकुशशिवात्मभूः ।
मायावर्म्मच घेघेउच्छिष्टायदहनाङ्गना ॥८५॥
द्वात्रिंशदरोमन्त्रोयजनंपूर्ववन्मतम् ।
रसे षुसप्तषट्षट्कनेत्रार्णैरङ्गमी रितम् ॥८६॥

84-86. Another Mantra is mentioned here It is of thirty two syllables. The Mantra is : Om Hasti Mukhāya Lambodarāya Ucchiṣṭa Mahātmane Ām Krom Hrīm Klīm Hrīm Hūm Ghe Ghe Ucchiṣṭāya Svāhā (Om to the elephant faced Lambodara, to the great soul Ucchiṣṭa Ām etc. and Śvāhā unto Ucchiṣṭa).

The details of worship etc. as before. The Ṣadaṅga Nyāsa is with syllables divided at the syllables 6,5,7,6,6 and 2.

नौका: मन्त्रान्तरमाह ॥ तारइति ॥ तार: ओं महात्माङ्गे-महात्मने ॥ पाशादियुक्तम्॥ आत्मभूःक्लीं ॥ मायाह्रीं वर्महूं ॥ दहनांगनास्वाहा ॥ स्वरूपमन्यत्॥ यथाओंहस्तिमुखायलम्बोदरायउच्छिष्टमहात्मनेआंक्रोंह्रींक्लींह्रीं- हूंघेघेउच्छिष्टायस्वाहा ॥८४॥ ॥८५॥

Naukā: 84-85. He cites another Mantra Tāra etc. Tāra means Om Maṅātmaṅe means Mahātmane (to the noble soul). If must be joined with Pāśa etc.

Ātmabhū = Klīm.

Māyā = Hrīm Varma = Hum

Dahanāṅganā = Svāhā

The other thing the form itself. Hence Mantra is..... "Om Hastimukhāya Lambodarāya Ucchiṣta Mahātmane Ām Krom Klīm Hrīm Hum Ghe Ghe Ucchiśtāyā Svahā" thirty two syllabled Mantra. Ṣaḍaṇga is mentioned by Rasa etc.

उच्छिष्टगजवक्रस्यमन्त्रेष्वेषुनशोधनम् ।
सिद्धादिचक्रंमासादेःप्राप्तास्तेसिद्धिदागुरोः ॥८७॥
मनवोऽमीसदागोप्यानप्रकाश्यायतःकुतः ।
परीक्षितायशिष्यायप्रदेयानिजसूनवे ॥८८॥

87-88. In all these mantras of Ucchiṣta Gaṇesa there is no necessity of Śodhana (Purification) of the Siddha and other Cakras or months etc. They can accord powers even as they are derived from the preceptor.

These Mantras are to be kept as great secrets always. They cannot be revealed to all and sundry. After due tests they can be handed over to one's own son or disciple.

मायात्रिमूर्तिचंद्रस्थौंपचान्तकहुताशनौ ।
तारादिशक्तिबीजान्तोमंत्रोयंचतुरक्षरः ॥८९॥
भार्गवो स्यमुनिश्छंदोविराट्शक्तिर्गणाधिपः ।
देवोमायाद्वितीयेतुशक्तिबीजेप्रकीर्तिते ॥९०॥
षड्दीर्घयुग्द्वि तीयेनताराद्येनषडङ्गकम् ।
विधायसावधानेनमनसासंस्मरेत्प्रभुम् ॥९१॥

89-91. Now another Mantra called Śakti Vināyaka is mentioned. It is of four syllables *viz.* Om Hrīm Grīm Hrim. The sage of this Mantra is Bhārgava. The metre is

Virāṭ. The deity is Śaktigaṇeśa. Māyā is Bīja Śakti and Grim is Bīja.

The Ṣadaṅganyasa is to be performed with the syllable Grīm together with six long vowels (Ā, Ī, Ū, E, AI and AḤ) and Om prefixed to each.

After performing all these attentively the devotee meditates on the lord.

नौका: शक्तिविनायकसंज्ञं मन्त्रातरमाह ।। मायेति ।। मायाह्रीं ।। पञ्चान्तहुताशनौगकररेफौ ।। त्रिमूर्तिचन्द्रस्थौ इकारानुस्वारयुक्तौ ।। तेनग्रींतारादिशक्तिबीजान्त: प्रणवादिर्मायाबीजान्त: ।।यथा।। ओं ह्रीं ग्रीं ह्रीं इति चतुर्वर्ण: ।।८९।।

नौका: देवइति ।। पूर्वेणसम्बध: ।। माया शक्ति: ।। द्वितीयंबीजम् ।।९०।।

नौका: षडङ्गमाह ।। षडिति ।। ओंग्रांहृत् ।। ओं ग्रींशिरइत्यादि ।।९१।।

Naukā: 89. The Mantras of Ucchiṣṭagaṇeśa have been mentioned in full. He now cites the Mantra called Śakti Vinā Yaka –

Māyā = Hrīm Pañcāntakahutāśanau means letters Ga and Ra.

Trimūrticandrasthau means having letter I and Anusvāra. Hence it becomes Grīm. Tārādi Śakti Bījānta means beginning with Praṇava and ending with Māyā Bīja. Hence the four letter Mantras is Om Hrīm Grīm Hrīm.

Naukā: 90. Deva goes with the previous word Māyā = Śakti Dvitīyam = Bījam.

Naukā: 91. Ṣaḍaṅga is mentioned Ṣaḍaṅga etc. Om Grām Hṛt Om Grīm Śirah etc.

विषाण कुशावक्षसूत्रंचपा शंदधानंकरैर्मोदकंपुष्करेण ।
स्वपत्न्यायुतंहेमभूषाभराढ्यंगणेशंसमुद्यद्दिनेशाभमीडे ।।९२।।

92. Dhyāna Verse :–

I adore (**and meditate** on) Gaṇeśa who holds goad and **garland** of rosaries in the right hands and tusk and noose in the left hands, who holds the sweet meat in his trunk, who has the lustre of the rising sun, who is fully bedecked in gold ornaments and who is accompanied by his wife.

एवंध्या त्वाजपेल्लक्षचतुष्कंतद्दशांशतः ।
अपूपैर्जुहुयाद्वह्नौमध्वक्तैस्तर्पयेच्चतम् ॥९३॥
पूर्वोक्तेपूजयेत्पीठके सरेष्वङ्गदेवताः ।
दलेषुवक्रतुण्डाद्यान्ब्राह्मीत्याद्यान्दलाग्रगान् ॥९४॥
ककुप्पालांस्तदस्त्राणिसिद्धएवंभवेन्मनुः ।

93-94½. The initiatory rite is as follows. After meditating thus the devotee shall repeat the Mantra four hundred thousand times. A tenth of that for Havana with sweet pies smeared with honey and then Tarpaṇa is to be performed. As mentioned before, on the pedestal in the filaments the devotee shall worship the subordinate deities. The worship of the deities Vakratuṇḍa etc. is in the petals, that of Brāhmī etc, at the tips of the petals and the guardians of the quarters and their weapons are to be worshipped in the respective quarters. Thus the Mantra becomes realized perfectly.

नौकाः ध्यानमाह॥ विषाणेति ॥ कुशाक्षसूत्रे दक्षयोः अन्येवापयोः ॥९२॥ ॥९३॥ ॥९४॥

Naukā: 92-94. Dhyāna is mentioned by Viṣāṇa etc. Goad and rosary thread in the right hands others in the left hands.

घृताक्तमन्नंजुहुयादावर्षादन्नवान्भवेत् ॥९५॥
परमान्नैर्हुताल क्ष्मीरिक्षुदंडैर्नृपश्रियः ।
रम्भाफलैर्नारिकेलैःपृथुकैर्वश्यताभवेत् ॥९६॥
घृतेनधनमाप्नोतिलवणैर्मधु संयुतैः ।
वामनेत्रांवशीकुर्य्यादपूपैःपृथिवीपतिम् ॥९७॥

95-97. The devotee shall perform Havana with cooked food smeared with ghee. Within a year he shall possess ample food grains.

If the Havana is performed with milk pudding the devotee gains glory and fortune.

With Sugarcane stalks he gains Royal glory, with bananas, coconuts and flattened rice he can control people, with ghee-he gains wealth; with salt in the company of honey he can captivate the hearts of damsels and with sweet pies he can gain the favour of the king

नौकाः ककुप्पालानिन्द्रादीन् ।।९५।।

नौकाः परमान्नंपायसम् ।।९६।।

नौकाः वामनेत्रानारी ।।९७।।

Naukā: 95. Kakuppālān means Indra and others.

Naukā: 96. Paramānnam means Milk pudding.

Naukā: 97. Vāma Netrā means women.

तारोरमाचन्द्रयुक्तःखान्तःसौम्यासमीरणः ।
ङेन्तोगणपतिस्तोयंरवरान्तेदसर्वच ।।९८।।
जनमेवशमादीर्घोवायुःपावककामिनी ।
अष्टाविंशतिव र्णोयंमनुर्द्धनसमृद्धिदः ।।९९।।
अन्तर्य्यामीमुनिश्छंदोगायत्रीदेवतामनोः ।
लक्ष्मीविनायकोबीजंर माशक्तिर्वसुप्रिया ।।१००।।

98-100. The next Mantra is twenty-eight syllabled Lakṣmī Vināyaka Mantra. It is as follows :–

"Om Śrīm Gam Saumyāya Gaṇapataye Varavarada Sarvajanam Me Vaśamānaya Svāhā" (Om unto the gentle Gaṇapati. O bestower of excellent boons, bring every one under my control (Svāhā). It bestows rich quantity of wealth, The sage of the Mantra is Antaryāmī (The immenent Soul). The metre is Gāyatrī. The deity of the

Mantra is Lakṣmī Vināyaka. The Bīja is Śrīm and the Śakti is Svāhā.

The Ṣaḍaṅga Nyāsa is to be performed with Śrī and Gam together with the six long vowels.

नौका: मंत्रांतरमाह । तारइति तार: ओं । रमाश्रीं ।। चन्द्रयुक्त: खान्त: गं ।। समीरणोय : ।। तोयंव : ।। दीर्घोन: ।। वायुर्य: ।। षावककामिनी स्वाहा।। अन्यत्यस्वरूंपम् ।। ओंश्रींगंसौम्या ।।

यगणपतयेवरवरदसर्वजनंमेवशमानयस्वाहेति अष्टाविंशत्यर्णोलक्ष्मी- गणेशोमन्त्र: ।।९८।। ।।९९।। ।।१००।।

Naukā: 98-100. He cites another Mantra Tāra etc. Tāra = Om Ramā = Śrīm.

Candrayukta Khānta means Gam

Samīraṇa = Ya | Toyam = Va

Dīrgha = Na | Vāyu = Ya

Pāvakakāmini = Svāhā

The other thing is the form itself

The Twenty eight syllabled Mantra named Lakṣmī Gaṇeśa is – "Om Śrīm Gam Saumyāya Gaṇapataye Vara Varada Sarva Janam Me Vaśam Ānaya Svāhā".

रमागणेशबीजाश्यांदीर्घाढ्याश्यांषडङ्गकम् ।
दन्ताभयेचक्रदरौदधानंकराग्रगस्वर्णघटंत्रिनेत्रम् ।
धृता ब्जयालिङ्गितमब्धिपुत्र्यालक्ष्मीगणेशंकनकाभमीडे ।।१०१।।

101. The Dhyāna Verse. I respectfully offer my obeisance to Lakṣmīgaṇeśa whose lustre is golden, who has three eyes, who holds tusk and conch shell in the right hands and the gesture of fearlessness and the discus in the left hands, in whose trunk there is the gold pot and who is embraced by the goddess Lakṣmī holding a lotus.

चतुर्लक्षंजपेन्मंत्रंसमिद्धिर्बिल्वशा खिन: ।
दशांशंजुहुयात्पीठे पूर्वोक्तेतंप्रपूजयेत् ।।१०२।।

आदावङ्गानिसंपूज्यशक्तीरष्टविमायजेत् ।
बलाकाविमलापश्चात्कमलावनमालिका ॥१०३॥
विभीषिकामालिकाचशाङ्करीवसुबालिका
शंखप द्मनिधीपूज्यौपाश्र्वयोर्दक्षवामयोः ॥१०४॥
लोकाधिपांस्तदस्त्राणितद्बहिःपरिपूजयेत् ।
एवंसिद्धेम नौमंत्रीप्रयोगान्कर्तुमर्हति ॥१०५॥

102-105. The procedure for initiatory rite. The devotee has to repeat the Mantra four hundred thousand times. With the twigs of the Bilva tree (wood apple) he has to perform Havana forty thousand times. Lakṣmī Vināyaka is to be worshipped in the pedestal mentioned before. At the outset he performs the Aagapūjā (ancillary worship) and then these eight Śaktis are worshipped.

The Śaktis are :—Balākā, Vimalā, Kamalā, Vanamālikā, Vibhīṣikā, Mālikā, Śāṅkarī and Vasubālikā.

The treasure troves Śaṅkha and Padma are to be worshipped on the right and left sides.

In the outside he guardians of the quarters and their weapons are worshipped.

When he has realised the Mantra thus the devotee can proceed with the rites for the sake of achieving cherished desires.

नौका: षडंगमाह ॥ रमेति ॥ श्रींगांहृत, श्रींगींशिरः, श्रूंगृशिखेत्यादि ॥ ध्यानमाह॥ दन्तेति ॥ दन्तेतिशङ्खौदक्षयोः ॥ अभय चक्रेवामयोः शुण्डाग्रेस्वर्णकुम्भः ॥१०१॥ ॥१०२॥ ॥१०३॥ ॥१०४॥ ॥१०५॥

Naukā: 101-105. Ṣaḍaṅga is mentioned Ramā etc. Śrim Gām Hṛt. Śrīmgīm Śiraḥ Śrīm Gūm Śikhā etc.

Dhyāna is referred to Danta etc. In the right hands tusk and conch shell. Gesture of fearlessness and discus in the left hands. The gold pot at the tip of the trunk.

उरोमात्रेजलेस्थित्वामंत्रीध्यात्वाकर्मण्डले ।
एवंत्रिलक्षंजपतो धनवृद्धिःप्रजायते ॥१०६॥

106. The devotee stands in water up to his chest and meditates on the deity in the solar disc. He repeats the Mantra three hundred thousand times. His wealth increases.

बिल्वमूलंसमास्थायतावज्जप्तेफलंहितत् ।
अशोककाष्ठैर्ज्वलितेवह्नावा ज्याक्तक्ततण्डुलैः ॥१०७॥
होमतोवशयेद्विश्वमर्ककाष्ठंशुचावपि ।
खादिराग्नौनरपतिंलक्ष्मींपायसहोमतः ॥१०८॥

107-108 The devotee sits at the root of the Bilva tree and repeats the mantra three hundred thousand times He reaps the same benefit as in the previous case.

By performing Havana with rice grains smeared with ghee in the fire kindled with Aśoka twigs, the devotee can bring the entire universe under his control. During the hot season Ārka twigs can be used.

If the Havana is performed with milk pudding in the fire kindled with Khādira twigs the devotee brings the king under his control. He obtain glory and fortune also.

वक्रकर्णेन्दुयु गृणान्तौडैकदंष्ट्रायमन्मथः ।
मायारमागजमुखोगणपान्तेभगीहरिः ॥१०९॥
वरवालाग्निसत्याः सरे फारूढंजलंस्थिरा ।
सेन्दुम्मेषोमेवशान्तेमानयोषर्बुधप्रिया ॥११०॥
स्यात्रयस्त्रिंशदर्णाढ्योमनुस्त्रैलो क्यमोहनः ।
गणकोस्यत्रृषिश्छंदोगायत्रीदेवतापुनः ॥१११॥
त्रैलोक्यमोहनकरोगणेशोभक्तसि द्धिदः ।
रविवेदशरोदन्वद्रसनेत्रैःषडङ्गकम् ॥११२॥

109-112 The Mantra Trailokya Mohana Gaṇeśa is as follows :–

Vakratuṇḍaika Daṁṣṭrāya Klīm Hrīm Śrīm Gam Gaṇapate Varavarada Sarvajanaṁ Me Vaśa Mānaya Svāhā (O Gaṇapati, Klīm Hrīm Śrīm Gam unto the curved mouthed single tusked deity. Get everyone under my control–Svāhā). This is the thirty three syllabled Mantra. The sage of this Mantra is Gaṇaka. The metre is Gāyatrī. The deity is Gaṇeśa who fascinates the three worlds. He bestows all powers to the devotees.

The Ṣaḍaṅganyāsa is to be performed with syllables divided at 12, 4, 5, 4, 6 and 2.

नौका: तावत्रिलक्षंतत्फलंधनवृद्धि: ॥१०७॥

Naukā: 107. Tāvat means that much *i.e.* three hundred thousand. Its benefit–increase in the wealth.

नौका: त्रैलोक्यमोहनगणेशमंत्रमाह ॥ वक्रेति ॥ स्वरूपम् ॥ णांतस्त: ॥ कर्णेंदुयुक् ॥ उबिंदुयुत: ॥ मन्मथ: क्लींमायाह्रीं ॥ रमा श्रीं ॥ गजमुखोंगं॥ भगीहरि: ॥ एयुतस्त: बालोव: ॥ अग्नीर: ॥ सत्योद: ॥ रेफारूढजलंर्व ॥ स्थिराद: ॥ सेन्दुर्मेष: नं ॥ उषर्बुधप्रियास्वाहा ॥ स्वरूपमन्यत् ॥ यथा॥ वक्रतुंडकदंष्ट्रायक्लींह्रीं॥ श्रीगंगणपते वरवरदसर्वजनंमेवशमान-यस्वाहेतित्रयस्त्रिंशद्वर्णा: ॥१०९॥ ॥११०॥ ॥१११॥

Naukā: 109-111. He cites Trailokyamohana Gaṇeśa Mantra–Vakta etc. It is form itself Ṇānta=Ta. Karnenduyukta means having Uand Anuswāra.

Manmatha = Klīm	Māyā = Hrīm
Ramā = Śrīm	Gajamukha = Ga
Bhagī Harī = Ta with E (*i.e.* Te)	
Bāla = Va	Agni = Ra
Satya = Da	Rephārūḍhajalam = Rva
Sthirā = Ja	Sendu Meṣ = Nam

Uṣarbudhapriyā = Svāhā. Other things form itself. Thus the thirty three syllabled Mantra is – "Vakra Tuṇḍaika Daṁṣṭrāya Klīm Hrīm Śrīm Gam Gaṇapate Vara Varada Sarvajanam Me Vaśamānaya Svāhā".

नौका: षडंगमाह ॥ रवीति ॥ उदन्वन्तश्चत्वार: ॥११२॥

Naukā: 112. He explains Ṣadaṅga Nyāsa Ravi etc.

Udanvantaḥ = four

गदाबीजपूरेधनुशूलचक्रेसरोजोत्पलेपाश धान्याग्रदन्तान् ।
करै: संदधानंस्वशुडाग्रराजन्मणीकुम्भमंकाधिरूढंस्वपत्न्या ॥११३॥
सरोजन्मनाभूषणानांभरेणोज्ज्वलद्धस्ततन्व्यासमालिङ्गिताङ्गम् ।
करीन्द्राननंचन्द्रचूडंत्रिनेत्रंजगन्मोहनं रक्तकान्तिंभजेत्तम् ॥११४॥

113-114. These two verses are inended for the Dhy‾ ıa. The devotee shall resort to the three eyed, world-fascinating red lustred lord who holds in his right-hands mace, pomegranate, trident, discus and lotus and in the left hands bow, lily, noose, ear of corn and the tusk, who has a shining bejewelled pot in his trunk, whose face resembles that of an elephant, who is moon-crested and who is embraced by his wife seated on his lap and shining with many ornaments with a lotus in her hand.

नौका: ध्यानमाह ॥ गदेति ॥ गदाबीजपूरशूलचक्रपद्मा निदक्षेषुअन्यान्यन्येषु॥ धान्याग्रंव्रीहिमंजरी ॥११३॥

Naukā: 113. Dhyāna is mentioned. In the right hands – Mace pomegrante, trident, discus and louts. The other things in the other hands.

Dhānyāgram = Ear of corn

वेदलक्षंजपेन्मंत्रमष्टद्रव्यैर्दशांशत: ।
हुत्वापूर्वोदितंपीठेपूजयेद्रणनाय कम् ॥११५॥

115. The Mantra has to be repeated four hundred thousand times. The Havana with the eight articles forty

thousand times. After the Havana the devotee worships Gaṇanāyaka in the pedestal in the manner mentioned before.

अङ्गार्च्चापूर्ववत्प्रोक्ताशक्तीः पत्रेषुपूजयेत् ।
वामाज्येष्ठाचरौद्रीस्यात्कालीकलपदा दिका ॥११६॥
विकरिण्याह्वयातद्वद्बलाद्या प्रमथन्यपि।
सर्वभूतदमन्याख्यामनोन्मन्यपिचाग्रतः ॥११७॥

116-117. The Ancillary worship is as before. He shall worship the Śaktis in the petals. They are Vāmā, Jyeṣṭhā Raudrī, Kalakālī, Balavikariṇī, Balapramathanī, Sarvabhūta Damanī and Manonmanī.

नौकाः किंभूतयापत्न्या ॥ सरोजन्मनापद्मेन भूषणसमूहेनचक्रमात् ॥ ज्वलन्दीप्यमानोहस्तीज्वलंतीतनुश्चयस्यास्तया ॥११४॥ ॥११५॥ ॥११६॥ ॥११७॥

Naukā: 114-117. How is the wife? Respectively by lotus and ornaments. Shinning hand and shining body—one who has that.

दिक्षुप्रमोदःसुमुखोदुर्मुखोविघ्ननाशकः ।
दीर्घाद्यामातरः पूज्याइंद्राद्याआयुधान्यपि ॥११८॥
एवंसिद्धेमनौकुर्य्यात्प्रयोगानिष्टसिद्धये ।

118-118½. In the four quarters Pramoda, Sumukha, Durmukha and Vighna Nāśaka are to be worshipped. The Mothers (Brāhmī etc.) are to be worshipped with long vowels prefixed.

Thereafter Indra and others as well as their weapons are to be worshipped.

After mastering the Mantra thus the devotee can proceed ahead with their performance for realizing cherished desires.

वशयेत्कमलैर्भूपान्मन्त्रिणःकुमुदैर्हुतैः ॥११९॥
समिद्भरैश्चलदलसमुद्भूतैर्द्धरासुरान् ।
उदुम्बरोत्थैर्नृपतीन्प्लक्षैर्वाटैर्विशोन्तिमान् ॥१२०॥
क्षौद्रेणक नकप्राप्तिर्गोप्राप्तिःपयसागवाम् ।
ऋद्धिर्दध्योदनैरन्नघृतैःश्रीर्वेतसैर्जलम् ॥१२१॥

119-121. If lotuses are used for Havana the devotee captivates kings and with lilies the Ministers.

By means of the twigs of Aśvattha tree he can captivate Brahmins; with those of Udumbara he can master kings; with the twigs of Plakṣa he can control Vaiśyas and with those of Vata the Śūdras.

By using honey for Havana he gets gold : by using Cow's milk he gets Cows; by using curd rice he gets prosperity, by using ghee he gets food and glory and by using vetasa (reed) he gets planty of water (*i.e.* good showers and perennial supply of water).

नौकाः दीर्घाद्यामातरः ॥ आंब्राह्ययैनमः ॥ ईंमाहेश्वर्यैनमइत्यादि ॥११८॥ ॥११९॥

Naukā: 118-119. Dīrghādyā Mātarah means the devotee shall say Ām Brāhmyai Namaḥ īm Māheśvaryai Namaḥ etc.

नौकाः चलदलोश्वत्थस्तस्यसमिद्भिधरा सुरान्विप्रान्वशयेत्॥ औदुंबरसमिद्भिर्नृपतीन्वशयेत् ॥ प्लक्षसमिद्भिर्वैश्यान् ॥ वटजाभिरंतिमान् शूद्रान् ॥१२०॥ ॥१२१॥

Naukā: 120-121. Caladala means Aśvatha (Holy fig tree) with its twigs. Dharāsurān means Brahmins. He shall control them so. He shall bring kings under control by the twigs of Udumbara. The Vaiśyas with Plakṣa twigs. The last ones *i.e.* Śūdras with twigs of Vaṭa (banyan).

तारोवर्मगणेशोभूर्हरिद्रागणलोहितः ।
आषाढीयेवरवरसत्यःसर्वजतर्जनी ॥१२२॥

हृदयंस्तम्भयद्वं द्वंवह्लभांस्वर्णरितसः ।
द्वात्रिंशदक्षरीमंत्रोमदनोमुनिरीरितः ॥१२३॥
छन्दोनुष्टुबूदेवतातुहरिद्राग णनायकः ।
वेदाष्टशरसप्ताङ्गनेत्रार्णैरङ्गमीरितम् ॥१२४॥

122-124. The Mantra of Haridrāgaṇapati is mentioned next. The thirty two syllabled Mantra is as follows :–

"Om Hum Gam Glaum Haridrāgaṇapati Vara Varda Sarvajanahṛdayam Stambhaya Stambhaya–Svāhā" (Om Hum Gam Glaum obeisance unto the lord Gaṇapati of turmeric. O bestower of excellent boons. Stun the hearts of all. Stun Svāhā). The sage of this Mantra is Madana; the metre is Anuṣtup; the deity is Haridrāgaṇanāyaka. The Ṣaḍaṅga Nyāsa is with syllables divided at 4, 8, 5, 7, 6 and 2.

नौकाः हरिद्रागणेशमनुमाह ॥ तारइति ॥ तार ओं ॥ वर्महुं ॥ गणेशागं भूःग्लौ ॥ लोहितःपः आषाढीतः ॥ सत्योदः ॥ तर्जनीनः स्वर्णरेतसोवह्लभा-स्वाहा॥ स्वरूपमन्यत् ॥ यथा-ओं हुंगलौहरिद्रागणपतयेवरदर-दसर्वजनहृदयंस्तंभयस्तंभय ॥ स्वाहेतिद्वात्रिंशद्वर्णः ॥१२२॥ ॥१२३॥

Naukā: 122-123. He mentions the Mantra of Haridrā Gaṇeśa by Tāra etc.

Tāra = Om	Varma = Hum
Gaṇeśa = Gam	Bhū = Glau
Lohita = Pa	Āśaḍhī = Ta
Satya = Da	Tarjanī = Na

Svarṇa Retasaḥ Vallabhā = Svāhā

The other things – form itself.

Then the 32 syllabled Mantra is :–

"Om Hum Gam Glaum Haridrāgaṇa pataye Vara Varada Sarvajana Hṛdayam Stambhaya Stambhaya Svāhā.

नौका: षडंगमाह ।। वेदेति ।।१२४।।

Naukā: 124. Ṣaḍaṅga is indicated by Veda etc.

पाशाङ्कुशौमोदकमेकदन्तंकरैर्दधानंक नकासनस्थम् ।
हारिद्रखण्डप्रतिमंत्रिनेत्रंपीतांशुकंरात्रिगणेशमीडे ।।१२५।।

125. This is the Dhyāna Verse. I worship Haridrā Gaṇeśa who holds goad and sweet meat in the right hand and the noose and tusk in the left hands, who is seated in the golden throne whose lustre is like that of turmeric, who has three eyes and who wears yellow cloth.

वेदलक्षंजपित्वान्तेह रिद्राचूर्णमिश्रितैः ।
दशांशंतण्डुलैर्हुत्वाब्राह्मणानपिभोजयेत् ।।१२६।।
पूर्वोक्तपीठेप्रयजेदङ्गमातृ दिशाधवैः ।
एवमाराधितोमंत्रस्सिद्धोयच्छेन्मनोरथान् ।।१२७।।

126-127. The devotee repeats this Mantra four hundred thousand times and performs forty thousand Havanas with rice grains mixed with powdered turmeric. Then he feeds Brahmins.

In the pedestal mentioned before he shall do the worship with the Ancillaries, mothers and guardians of the quarters. The Mantra thus propitiated shall bestow all the cherished desires.

शुक्लपक्षेचतुर्थ्यांतुकन्यापिष्टहरि द्रया ।
विलिप्यांगंजलेस्नात्वापूजयेद्गणनायकम् ।।१२८।।

128. On the fourth day of the bright half, the devotee shall smear his body with turmeric powdered by a maiden. Then he shall take bath in (holy) water and then worship Gaṇanāyaka.

तर्पयित्वापुरस्तस्यसहस्त्रंसाष्टकंजपेत् ।
शतंहुत्वाघृतापूपैर्भोजयेद्ब्रह्मचारिणः ॥१२९॥
कुमारीरपि संतोष्यगुरुंप्राप्नोतिवांछितम् ।
लाजैःकन्यामवाप्नोतिकन्यापिलभतेवरम् ॥१३०॥

129-130. After performing Tarpaṇa he shall repeat the Mantra thousand and eight times. He then performs Havana with sweet pies prepared in ghee a hundred times. Then he shall feed religious students and propitiate virgins. He then realises even his greatest desires. He shall propitiate his preceptor too. If the Havana is performed with fried grain he gets a bride and the bride too get a bridegroom.

वंध्यानारीरज स्नातापूजयित्वागणाधिपम् ।
पलप्रमाणगोमूत्रेपिष्टासिंधुवचानिशाः ॥१३१॥
सहस्त्रमंत्रयेत्कन्याबटू न्तसभोज्यमोदकैः ।
पित्वातदौषधंपुत्रंलभतेगुणसागरम् ॥१३२॥
वाणीस्तम्भंरिपुस्तम्भंकुर्या न्मनुरुपासितः ।
जलग्निचौरसिंहास्त्रप्रमुखानपिरोधयेत् ॥१३३॥

131-133. The barren lady shall worship Gaṇādhipa after her menstrural period after due bath. She then takes a Pala of Cow's urine and soaks turmeric and the aromatic root Vacā. Then she inspires it with the repititions of the mantra a thousand times. She then feeds virgins and religious students. Thereafter she shall drink that concoction. She is sure to get a virtuous son.

By mastering this Mantra duly the devotee can conques water, fire, thieves, lions and weapons by with standing them. He can stun the speech of enemies also.

नौकाः ध्यानमाह ॥ पाशेति ॥ अंकुशमोदकौदक्षयोः ॥ पशदन्तावन्ययोः ॥

रात्रिगणशोहरिद्रागणपतिः ॥१२५॥ ॥१२६॥ ॥१२७॥ ॥१२८॥ ॥१२९॥

Naukā: 125-129. Dhyāna is mentioned.

Goad and sweetmeat in the right hands. The noose and the tusk in the others Rātrigaṇeśa means Haridrā Gaṇapati.

नौका: कुमारीरपीति ॥ भोजयेदित्यनेनान्वेति ॥१३०॥ ॥१३१॥ ॥१३२॥ ॥१३३॥

Naukā: 130-133. Kumārīrapi etc. It goes with "he should feed".

शार्ङ्गीमांसस्थितःसेंदुर्बीजमु क्तंगणेशितुः ।
हरिद्राख्यस्ययजनंपूर्ववत्प्रोदितंमनोः ॥१३४॥
प्रोक्त एतेगणेशस्यमंत्राइष्टमभीप्सता ।
गोपनीयानदुष्टेश्योवदनीयाः कथंचन ॥१३५॥

134-135. The Bījā of Gaṇapati is Glam. The initiatory of this Mantra is as before.

These Mantras of Gaṇeśa mentioned here are to be kept as great secret by a person who desires cherished desires. He should not mention them to wicked people.

इति श्रीमहीधरविरचितेमंत्रमहोदधौगणेशमंत्रकथनंनामद्वितीयस्तरंगः॥२॥

नौका: मंत्रांतरमाह ॥ शार्ङ्गीति ॥ शार्ङ्गीगः ॥ मांसस्थितःलकारस्थः ॥ ग्लमितबीजं। हरिद्रागणपतिः पूजनंपूर्ववत् ॥१३४॥

Naukā: 134. He mentions another Mantra with Śārṅgi etc.

Śārṅgi = Ga

Māsasthita = Stationed in the letter La. Glum is the Bīja. The worship of Haridrā Gaṇapati is as before.

Thus the second Taraṅga named Narration of the Mantras of Gaṇeśa comes to a close in the commentary Naukā of Mantra Mahodadhi.

इतिमंत्रमहोदधि० नौकायांगणशेमंत्रकथन नामद्वितीयस्तरङ्गः ॥२॥

Notes

4. The procedure for the Ṣaḍaṅga Nyāsa: -

The devotee says Om Vam obeisance to the thumbs obeisance—obeisance to the heart.

Om Kram obeisance to the index fingers obeisance Svāhā unto the head.

Om Tum obeisance to the middle fingers obeisance—Vaṣaṭ unto the tuft.

Om Ḍām obeisance to the ring fingers obeisance—Hum unto armour.

Om Yam obeisance to the little fingers obeisance— Vauṣaṭ unto the three eyes.

Om Dadita obeisance to the index fingers Svāhā to the head.

Om Nidhido Ratnadhātumān obeisance to the middle fingers Vaṣat to the tuft.

Om Rakṣohaṇo obeisance to the ring fingers. Hum unto the Armour.

Om Balagahano obeisance to the little fingers Vauṣ aṭ to the three eyes.

Om Vakratuṇḍāya Hum obeisance to the palms and the backs of the hands. Phaṭ unto the Astra.

Dhyāna—Verse 6.

The number of Japas is 600,000.

35-39. The Nyāsa of the Mantra of Ucchiṣṭa Ganapati as before with the respective parts of the Mantra.

The procedure of the Adoration as in the previous with the new names mentioned here substituted for the old names.

In all the subsequent Mantras also the procedure is the same. Wherever new names are given to the Śaktis etc. in the original Verses, those names are respectively substituted.

Mantras to Hanumān

अधोच्यंतेहनुमतोमन्त्राः सर्वेष्टसिद्धये ।
इन्द्रस्वरेंदुसंयुक्तोवराहोहसफाग्नयः ॥१॥
झिंटीशबिंदुसंयुक्ताद्वि तीयंबीजमीरिम् ।
गदीपांताग्निरुद्रेन्दुसंयुतःस्यात्तृतीयकम् ॥२॥
हसरामनुंचंद्राढ्याश्चतुर्थंहसखाः फरा ।
शिवेंद्राढ्याः पंचमः स्याद्धसौमन्बिदुगौपरम् ॥३॥
ङेयुतोहनुमान्हार्दमंत्रोयंद्वादशाक्षरः ।
रामचंद्रोमुनिश्चास्यजगतीछंदईरितम् ॥४॥
हनुमान्देवताबीजं षष्ठंशक्तिद्वितीयकम् ।
षड्बीजैरंगषट्कंस्यान्मूर्ध्निभालेदृशोर्मुखे ॥५॥
कंठेचबाहुद्वितये हृदिकुक्षौ चनाभितः ।
लिंगेजानुद्वयेपादद्वयेवर्णान्क्रमान्न्यसेत् ॥६॥
षड्वीजानिपदद्वंद्वेमूर्ध्निभालेमुखेहृदि ।
नाभावूर्वोर्जंघयोश्चपादयोर्विन्यसेत्क्रमात् ॥७॥

1-7. For the sake of the realization of all cherished desires, the Mantras of Hanumān are being explained.

The twelve syllabled Mantra consists of six Bījas and Hanumate Namaḥ.

The first Bīja is Haum, II. Hsphrem, III. Khphrem, IV. Hsraum, V. Hskhphrem, and VI. Hsaum.

The sage of this Mantra is Rāmacandra, the metre is Jagatī and the deity is Hanumān. The sixth Bīja is the Bīja of the whole Mantra and the second Bīja is Śakti.

Saḍaṅga Nyāsa. This is to be performed by means of the Bījas one by one.

Varṇa Nyāsa. The letters of the Mantra are used one by one for the following Varṇa Nyāsa as follows :—head, forehead, eyes, mouth, throat, the two arms, heart, belly, navel, penis, the two knees and the two feet.

Pada Nyāsa. The six Bījas and last two words Hanumate and Namaḥ are used for Pada Nyāsa in the following order— head, forehead, mouth, heart, navel, thighs, calves and feet.

नौका: श्रीहनुमतो मंत्रान्वक्तुंप्रतिजानीते ।। अथेति ।। मंत्रमुद्धरति ।। इंद्रेति ।। वाराहोह: इंद्रस्वरऔबिंदुस्ताभ्यांयुत:हौं ।। हसफस्वरूपम् ।। अग्नीर: एते ।।१।।

नौका: झिंठीशबिंदुयुता: एबिंदुयुता: ।। तेनहस्फ्रें ।। गदीख: ।। पांताग्निरुद्रेंदुयुत: ।। पांत:फ:अग्नीररुद्रए ।। इंदुर्बिंदु:तैर्युत: ।। ख्फ्रं ।।२।।

नौका: हसरा मनुचंद्राढ्या: औबिंदुयुता ह्स्त्रौं ।। हसखफरा: शिर्बेद्वाढ्या:एबिंदुयुता: ।। तेनह्स्ख्फ्रें ।। हसौमन्बिन्दुगौ औबिंदुयुतौ हूसौं ।। परंतत: ।।३।।

नौका: ङ़ेयुतोहनुमान्मनुमते ।। हार्दंनम: ।। यथा–हौंहस्फ्रेंख्फ्रेंहस्त्रौंह्स्ख्फ्रेंह्सौहनु-मतेनम: ।।४।।

नौका: षष्ठंह्सौमितिबीजं ।। द्वितीयेंह्स्फ्रेंमितिश क्ति: ।। हौंहृत् ।। ह्स्फ्रेंशिर: ।। ख्फ्रेंशिखेत्यादि० ।। वर्णन्यासमाह ।। मूर्ध्नीति ।। एकैकंसर्वत्र० ।।५-६।।

नौका: पदन्यासमाह ।। षडिति ।।

पदद्वंद्वंहनुमतेनमहति ।।७।।

Naukā: 1. He proclaims his intention to explain the Mantras of Śrī Hanumān. He analyses the Mantra.

Varāha = Ha

Indrasvara = Au

That with Indu = Haum

Hasapha — form itself

Agni = Ra

Naukā: 2. Jhiṇṭīśa Binduyutāḥ=having E, M Hence Hsphrem

Gadī=Kha

Pānta=Pha

Agni=Ra

Rudra=E

Indu=Bindu (M). Hence Khphrem.

Naukā: 3. Ha Sa Ra with Manu, Candra *i.e.* Au–M.

Hence Hsraum

Ha Sa Kha Pha Ra with Śiva and Indu. Hence Hskhphrem.

Ha Sa with manu and Indu–Hsaum. After that.

Naukā: 4. Neyuta Hanumān–Hanumate

Hārdam=Namaḥ e.g.

Haum, Hsphrem, Khphrem, Hsraum Hskhphrem, Hsaum Hanumate Namaḥ.

Naukā: 5-6. The sixth one *i.e.* Hsaum is Bīja. The second one *i.e.* Hsphrem is Śakti.

Hraum–obeisance to the heart

Hsphrem Svāhā unto the head Khphrem

Vaṣaṭ unto the tuft etc.

He explains Varṇanyāsa–one by one everywhere.

Naukā: 7. He explains Padanyāsa–Ṣaḍ etc.

The two words–Hanumate and Namaḥ.

बालार्कायुततेजसंत्रिभुवनप्रक्षोभकंसुन्दरंसुग्रीवादि समस्त-
वानरगणैःसंसेव्यपादाम्बुजम् ।

नादेनैवसमस्तराक्षसगणान्संत्रासयंतं प्रभुश्रीमद्रामपदांबुजस्मृ
तिरतध्यायामिवातात्मजम् ॥८॥

8. *Dhyāna Verse.* I meditate on the handsome son of the god of wind, who has the lustre of ten thousand rising suns, who stris up the three words, whose lotus like feet

are worthy of being served by Sugrīva and the entire hosts of the Monkeys, who terrifies the entire army of the Rākṣ aś as through his roaring sound alone and who is engaged in remembering the lotus like feet of Lord Śrī Rāmacandra.

एवंध्यात्वापेदर्कसहस्त्रंजितमानसः ।

दशांशंजुहुयाद्व्रीहीन्पयो दध्याज्यसंयुतान् ॥९॥

9. After meditating thus the devotee repeats the Mantra twelve thousand times with perfect control of the mind. He shall perform one thousand and two hundred Homas with cereals soaked in milk curds and ghee.

नौकाः ध्यानमाह ॥ बालेति ॥ वातात्मजंहनुमंतम् ॥८॥ ॥९॥

Naukā: 8-9. He explains Dhyāna–Bāla etc.

Vātātmajam–Hanuman.

विमलादियुतेपीठेपूजाकार्य्याहनूमतः ।

केसरेष्वंगपूजास्याद्दलेष्वन्यांस्तदाह्वयान् ॥१०॥

10. The worship of Hanumān is to be performed in the pedestal having Vimalā etc. (as Śaktis) The six Aṅgas are to be worshipped in the filaments and the petals are to be used for adoring Hanumān with the following appellations.

नौकाः दलेषुतदाह्वयान् हनुमन्नामानि ॥१०॥

Naukā: 10. In the petals. His names - Hanumān's names.

रामभ क्तोमहातेजाकपिराजोमहाबलः ।

द्रोणाद्रिहारकोमेरुपीठकार्चनकारकः ॥११॥

दक्षिणाशाभास्क रश्चसर्वविघ्ननिवारकः ।

एवंनामानिसंपूज्यदलाग्रेषुचवानरान् ॥१२॥

सुग्रीवमंगदंनीलंजांबवंतं नलंतथा ।

सुषेणंद्विविदंमैंदंपूजयेद्दिक्पतीनपि ॥१३॥

11-13. They are (1) Rāmabhakta (devotee of Rāma), (2) Mahātejāḥ (of great splendour), (3) Kapirāja (king of Monkeys), (4) Mahābala (of great might), (5) Droṇādri Hāraka (one who carried and brought the mountain Droṇa), (6) Merupīṭhārcana Kāraka (one worships the Merupīṭha), (7) Dakṣiṇāśābhāskara (The Sun of the Southern quarter), (8) Sarvavighna Nivāraka (one who removes all obstacles).

Thereafter he shall worship on the tips of the petals the following monkeys–Sugrīva, Aṅgada, Nīla, Jāmbavān, Nala, Suṣeṇa, Dvivida and Mainda.

After that the devotee worships the guardians of the quarters.

एवंसिद्धेमनौमंत्रीस्वपरेष्टंप्रसाधयेत् ।
कद लीबीजपूराम्रफलैर्हुत्वासहस्त्रकम् ॥१४॥
द्वाविंशांतेब्रह्मचारिविप्रान्संभोजयेदथ ।
एवंकृतेमहाभूतवि षचौराद्युपद्रवाः ॥१५॥
नश्यंतिक्षणमात्रेणविद्वेषिग्रहदानवाः ।
अष्टोत्तरशतंवारि मंत्रितंविषना शनम् ॥१६॥

14-16 *Rites for realization of desires.* Having perfectly realized the Mantra, the devotee can accomplish the realization of this own as well as others' desires.

He shall perform a thusand Homas with the fruits of Banana, pomegranate and mango. Then he shall feed twenty two brahmin religious students leading celebate life. If this is done all the harassments due to great evil spirits, poisons and thieves and the like perish instantaneously. So also in the case of adverse planets and demons.

Water inspired with this Mantra one hundred and eight times, is destructive of poisons.

रात्रोनवशतंमंत्रजपेद्दशदिनाविधि ।
योनरस्तस्यनश्यंतिराजशत्रूत्थभीतयः ॥१७॥

17. The devotee shall repeat this Mantra nine hundred times everyday at night for ten days. He can thereby ward off the fear from kings and enemies.

अभिचारोत्थभूतोत्थज्वरेतन्मंत्रितैर्जलैः ।
भस्मभिःसलिलैर्वापिताडयेज्ज्वरिणःक्रुधा ॥१८॥
दिनत्रयाज्ज्वरान्मुक्तःससुखंलभतेनरः ।
तन्मंत्रितौषधंजग्ध्वानीरोगोजायतेध्रुवम् ॥१९॥

18-19. If fever is caused by black magic or evil spirits the exorciser shall angrily strike, the patient with water and holy ashes inspired with the Mantra. The patient gets relief from the fever within three days and becomes happy.

One who takes in the medicine inspired with the Mantra certainly gets rid of all ailments.

तन्मं त्रितंपयःपीत्वायोद्धुंगछेन्मनुंजपन् ।
तज्जप्तभस्मलिप्तांगः शस्त्रसंघैर्नबाध्यते ॥२०॥

20. The warrior must go to fight in battle after drinking the milk inspired by the Mantra repeating the Mantra to himself. If he smears himself with the holy ashes inspired by the Mantra he is not afficted by weapons of war.

नौकाः तानाह ॥ रामभक्तइत्यादि ॥११-२०॥

Naukā: 11-20. The names are Rāmabhakta etc.

शस्त्रक्षतंव्रणः शोफोलूतास्फोटोपिभस्मना ।
त्रिमंत्रितेनसंस्पृष्टाःशुष्यंत्यचिरतोनृणाम् ॥२१॥

21. Wounds from the weapons, cuts and bruises, tumour, boils due to spider poison etc. in the case of men

quickly become healed if the holy ashes inspired thrice by means of the Mantra are applied.

सूर्य्या स्तमयमारश्यजपेत्यसूर्योदयावधि ।
कीलकंभस्मचादायसप्ताहावधिसंयतः ॥२२॥
निखनेद्भस्मकी लौतौविद्विषांद्वार्य्यलक्षितम् ।
विद्वेषंमिथआपन्नाःपलायंतेऽरयोऽचिरात् ॥२३॥

22-23. The devotee shall begin to repeat the Mantra at dusk and continue till sunrise with a nail and holy ashes in his hands. With great continence he shall continue this for seven days. Without being observed he shall go to the portals of the enemies and bury the ashes and the nail there. Erelong the enemies get split due to mutual quarrel and flee the place.

नौकाः शस्त्रक्षतादयोवारत्रयमंत्रितेनभस्मनामार्जिताअचिराच्छुष्यंतिनश्यंति ॥२१-२३॥

Naukā: 21-23. The wounds from missiles etc. should be smeared with the ashes three times inspired with Mantra. Then they become healed.

अभिमंत्रितभ स्माम्बुदेहचंदनसंयुतम् ।
खाद्यादियोजितंयस्मैदीयतेसचदासवत् ॥२४॥

24. If a person scrapes off the sandal paste smeared over his body and dissolves it in water along with ashes inspired by the Mantra and mixes the solation with food stuffs for anyone to eat, that person shall be a slave unto him.

नौकाः देहचंदनंदेहेधृतंयच्चंदनंतेनयुतंभस्मांबुचमंत्रितंयस्मैदीयतेसवश्यःस्यात् ॥२४॥

Naukā: 24. Dehacandanam—The sandal paste applied over the body. The ashes mixed with it. If given to a person he shall become subject to control.

क्रूराश्चजंतवोनेनभवंति विधिनावशाः ।
ईशानदिक्स्थमूलेनभूतांकुशतरोः शुभाम् ॥२५॥
अंगुष्ठमात्रांप्रतिमांप्रविधायह नूमतः ।
प्राणसंस्थापनंकृत्वासिंदूरैःपरिपूज्यच ॥२६॥
गृहस्याभिमुखेद्वारेनिखनेन्मंत्रमुच्चरन् ।
भूताभिचारचौराग्निविषरोगनृपोद्भवाः ॥२७॥
संजायंतेगृहेतस्मिन्नकदाचिदुपद्रवाः ।
प्रत्यहंधन पुत्राद्यैरेधतेतद्गृहंचिरम् ॥२८॥

25-28. Cruel beasts of pray too become well controlled through this means.

The devotee shall make a nice image (of the size of the thumb) of Hanumān out of the south-east root of Bhūtāṅkuśa tree (Karañja or Ariṣṭa) and shall instil vital airs therein. The image shall be worshipped with saffron and then bury it in front of the house repeating the Mantra. Never can there be the harassment in this house brought about by evil spirits black magic, thieves, fire, poison, ailments and (tyrannous) kings.

That house shall flourish everyday with wealth and progeny for a long time.

निशिश्मशानभूमिस्थौभस्मनामृत्स्नयापिवा ।
शत्रोः प्रतिंकृतिंकृत्वाहृदिनामसमालिखेत् ॥२९॥
कृपप्राणप्रतिष्ठंतांभिंद्याच्छस्त्रैर्मनुंजपन् ।
मंत्रांतेप्रोच्चरेच्छत्रोर्नामछिंधिचभिंधिच ॥३०॥
मारयेतिचत स्यांदंतैरोष्ठंनिपीड्यच ।
पाण्योस्तलेप्रपीड्याथत्यक्त्वातांसदनंव्रजेत् ॥३१॥
एवंसप्तदिनंकुर्वन्ह न्याच्छत्रुंशिवावितम् ।
अर्द्धचंद्राकृतौकुंडेस्थंडिलेवाहुतंचरेत् ॥३२॥

मुक्तकेशः श्मशानस्थेलवणैरा जिकायुतैः ।
उन्मत्तफलपुष्पैश्चनखरोमविषैरपि ॥३३॥
काककौशिकगृध्राणांपक्षैःश्लेष्मातकाक्षजै ।
समिद्वरैश्चत्रिशतंदक्षिणाशामुखोनिशि ॥३४॥
सप्तघस्त्रानिंदकुर्वन्मारयेद्रिपुमुद्धतम् ।

29-34½. The devotee shall make an image of his enemy with ashes or clay at night, seated in the cremation ground. His name shall be written in the heart. The image is then instilled with vital airs. Repeating the Mantra he shall pierce the image with weapons. When the Mantra is concluded he shall utter the name of his enemy as well as the words – "Chindhi" (cut) "Bhindhi" (pierce) and Māraya (kill). After completing it he shall bite his upper lip with his teeth. He shall press his own palms with force and leave off the remnents of the image there. After that he shall go home. Doing like this for seven days he will be able to effect the death of his enemy even if he were to be guarded by Śiva.

The devotee has to perform Homas in a crescent shaped pit or on the ground of the cremation ground with his tuft kept loose. The articles for the Homa shall be salt mixed with mustard, the fruits and flowers of Dhattura, nails, hairs, poisonous stuffs, feathers of cow, owl and vulture, excellent twigs of Śleṣmātaka and Akṣa. At night he shall perform three hundred Homas facing the south. Continuing this rite, continuously for seven days he can bring about the death of even a haughty enemy.

नौकाः ईशानेत्यादितद्गृहंचिरमित्यंतएकः प्रयोगः ॥ भूतांकुशतरोःकरंजस्य अरिष्टस्यईशानदिशि स्थितेनमूलेनांगुष्ठमितांहनुमत्प्रतिमांकृत्वाप्राणान्संस्थाप्यसिंदूरैरभ्यर्च्चयद्गृहद्वारिनिखन्यतेतत्रसर्वोपद्रवनाशस्तद्वृद्धिश्च ॥२५-३१॥

Naukā: 25-31. Beginning with Īśāna etc. (verse 25) and ending with Tad Gṛham Ciram (verse 28) This constitutes one rite.

Bhūtāṁkuśataroḥ—of the tree Karañja or Ariṣṭa. With the root in the north-east side, the devotee shall make Hanumān's image of the size of the thumb. Then it shall be inspilled with vital airs and worshipped with saffron. If the image is buried in a house, all calamities perish there and the house flourishes.

शत षट्कंजपेद्रात्रौश्मशानेदिवसत्रयम् ॥३५॥
ततोवेतालउत्थायवदेद्भाविशुभाशुभम् ।
उदितंकुरुतेसः वँकिंकरीभूयमंत्रिणः ॥३६॥

35-36. For three days the devotee shall continue to repeat the Mantra at night in the cremation ground. Then a vampire shall come up and tell him what would happen whether favourable or otherwise. He shall become a servant of the devotee and carryout his behests.

हनुमत्प्रतिमांभूमौविलिखेत्तत्पुरोमनून् ।
साध्यनामद्वितीयांतंविमोचयविमोचय ॥३७॥
तत्सर्वंमार्जयेद्वाम हस्तेनाथपुनर्लिखेत् ।
एवमष्टोत्तरशतंलिखित्वामार्जयेत्पुनः ॥३८॥
एवंकृतेपराधीनोमुच्यतेनिग डात्क्षणात् ।
एवंविषेणादीनिकुर्यात्तत्पल्लवंलिखन् ॥३९॥

37-39. The devotee shall draw the figure of Hanumān on the ground and write the Mantras in front. Then he shall write the name of the concerned person in the accusative case and write Vimocaya Vimocaya thereafter (meaning—release release). Then he shall wipe off everything with the left hand and right them all over again. He shall thus write and wipe off one hundred and eight times. If this rite is duly performed the hapless dependent gets released from the fetters instantaneously.

Thus he can bring about hatred etc. by writing the

words to that effect.

नौका: शिवावितं शिवेनापिरक्षितंशत्रुमेवंकुर्वन्हन्यात् ।। अर्द्धचंद्रेत्यादिरिपुमुद्धत-मित्यंतएकोमारणप्रयोग: ।। उन्मत्तोधत्तूर श्लेष्मातक श्चिक्कणफलोवृक्ष: ।। अक्षोबिभीतकस्तदुत्थसमिद्भिश्चहुतंचरेज्जुमुयात्सप्तघस्नान् दिवसान् ।।३२-३८।।

Naukā: 32-38. Śivāvitam—protected even by Śiva. If the devotee does like this he shall kill his enemy.

Beginning with Ardhacandra etc (verse 32) and ending with Ripum Uddhatam (verse 35) is one rite for killing [Māraṇa rite].

Unmatta=Dhattūra. Śeṣmātaka is a tree with smooth unctuous fruit.

Akṣa=Bibhītaka. The devotee shall perform Homas with the twigs of that tree.

Saptaghasrān=seven days.

वश्यार्थेसर्षपैर्होमोविद्वेषेकरवीरजै: ।
कुसुमैरिध्मकाष्ठैर्वाजीरकैर्मरिचैरपि ।।४०।।
ज्वरेदूर्वागुडूचीभिर्दध्नाक्षीरेणवाघृतै: ।
शूलेहोम:कुबेरा क्षैरेरंडसमिधातथा ।।४१।।
तैलाक्ताभिश्चनिर्गुंडीसमिद्भिर्वाप्रयत्नत: ।
सौभाग्येचंदनैश्चंद्रैरोचनै लालवंगकै: ।।४२।।
सुगंधिपुष्पैर्वस्त्राप्त्यैतत्तद्धान्यैस्तदाप्तये ।
तत्पादरजसाराजीलवणाक्तेनमृत्य वे ।।४३।।

40-43. For the purpose of enchanting and alluring persons the Homa should be performed with Mustard. For the purpose of alienating persons the Homa should be with the flowers or twigs of Karavīra or with cummin seeds or pepper.

In the case of fever the Homas shall be scrupulously performed with Dūrvā, Guḍūcī, curds, milk or ghee.

In the case of acute pain the Homa shall be with Kuberākṣa (a variety of Tiktakṣupā) and Eraṇḍa twigs or with Nirguṇḍī twigs smearned with oil.

For the purpose of blissful buck the Homa shall be with sandal paste, camphor, rocana; cardamon, and claves.

For the purpose of getting good garments one should perform Homas with fragrant flowers and for getting the different kinds of grains the Homa shall be performed with the same grain.

For the purpose of killing the Homa shall be with the dust from the feet of the intended victim mixed with salt and mustard.

नौकाः पराधीनोबद्धोनिगडाच्छंखलातोमुच्यते ।। विद्वेषणादीनिविद्वेषमारणोच्चाटान्तत्कृतपल्लवंलिखन्नेवंकुर्यात् ।। अमुकंद्वे षय २ इतिद्वेष्ये मारय २ इतिमारणे इत्यादिपल्लवलेखनम् ।।३९-४०।।

नौकाः कुबेराक्षःसूक्ष्मकणस्तिक्तक्षुपाविशेषः ।।४१।। ।।४२।।

Naukā: 39-40. Parādhīna - bound—he is released from fetters. The case of alienation etc. alienation, killing, driving. For that purpose the requisite Pallava (Explanatory Phrase etc.) should be written and the rite shall be performed in this manner. "Alienate so and so" in the case of alienation "kill so and so" in the case of killing etc. etc.

Naukā: 41-42. Kuberākṣa is a shrub with very small seeds bitter in taste.

किंबहूक्तैर्विषेव्याधौशांतौमोहेचमारणे ।
विवादेस्तंभनेद्यूतभूतभीतोचसंकटे ।।४४।।
वश्येयुद्धेनृपद्वारेसमरेचौरसंकटे ।
मंत्रोयंसाधितोदद्यादिष्टसिद्धिंध्रुवंनृणाम् ।।४५।।

44-45. Why tell much? In all cases of poisoning quickness, peacemaking, fasinating, bringing about death, disputation, stupefying, fear from gambling and evil spirits, bewildering calamities, alluring activities, fighting, difficulties at the portals of the royal palace, battlefield, harassment of thieves and the like, this Mantra, effectively practised, shall bestow the fulfilment of cherished desires certainly unto all people.

नौका: यद्धान्यैर्होमस्तदाप्ति: ।। राजीलवणयुतेनयत्पादरजसाहूयतेसम्रियते ।।४३-४५।।

Naukā: 43-45. The devotee shall acquire that grain in plenty with which he performs Homas. That man is sure to die, the dust from whose foot is used for Homa along with Mustard and Salt.

वक्ष्येहनुमतोयंत्रंसर्वसिद्धिप्रदायकम् ।
वलयत्रितयंलेख्यंपुच्छकारसमन्वितम् ।।४६।।

46. I shall now explain the Yantra of Hanumān. It bestows all supernatural powers. Three spiralling circles resembling tail should be drawn.

साध्यनाम लिखेन्मध्येपाशबीजप्रवेष्टितम् ।
उपर्य्यष्टदलंकृत्वावर्मपत्रेषुसंलिखेत् ।।४७।।
वलयंबहिरालिख्यत द्बहिश्चतुरस्त्रकम् ।
चतुरस्त्रस्यरेखाग्रेत्रिशूलानिसमालिखेत् ।।४८।।
भूपुरस्याष्टवज्रेषुहूसौबीजंलिखे त्ततः ।
कोणेष्वंकुशमालिख्यमालामंत्रेणवेष्टयेत् ।।४९।।
तत्सर्ववेष्टयेद्यंत्रंवलयत्रितयेनच ।
वस्त्रेशि लायांफलकेताम्रपात्रेथकुड्यके ।।५०।।
भूर्जेवातांडपत्रेवारोचनानाभिकुंकुमैः ।
यंत्रमेतत्समालिख्य त्यक्ताशोब्रह्मचर्य्यवान् ।।५१।।
कपे:प्राणान्प्रतिष्ठाप्यपूजयेत्तंयथाविधि ।
सर्वदु:खनिवृत्यैतद्यंत्रमा त्मनिधारयेत् ।।५२।।
ज्वरमार्य्यभिचारघ्नंसर्वोपद्रवशांतिकृत् ।
योषितामपिबालानांधृतंजनमनो हरम् ।।५३।।

47-53. The name of the intended victim shall be written in the inner circle and it shall be surrounded by Pāśabīja (Ām).

An eight petalled lotus shall be described all round and Hum shall be written in all the petals. The circle should be described outside and the square outside that. At the points of the sides of the square the devotee writes trident figures. In the eight Vajras (inner cardinal edges) of the square he shall write the Bīja "Hsaum". In the outer corners Aṅkuśa (Krom) is written. The whole thing is then enveloped by the "Mūlāmantra" (to beexplained presently.

This Yantra (Mystic diagram) is then circumscribed squares with three parallel lines on all sides.

This Yantra can be written on a cloth, rock slab, wooden plank, copper plate, Bhūrja bark, palm leaf or on the wall with Rocana orpiment, musk and saffron.

After writing the diagram duly the devotee shall observe the vow of celebacy and should not entertain any special craving. He should observe fast too. In this manner he shall instil the vital airs into it and duly worship it.

For the purpose of eradicating all miseries the devotee shall wear that Yantra as an amulet.

This Yantra is destructive of fever, plague and pestilence and black magic. It quells all types of harassments. It it is worn by children and women it delights then adequetely.

नौका: मन्त्रमाह ।। वलयेति ।। पुच्छाकारंवलयत्रयविलिख्यमध्ये-आमितिबीजेनवेष्टितंसाध्यनामलिखेत् ।। तदुपर्यष्टदलेषुहुमिति ।।४६।। ।।४७।।

नौका: बहिरेकंवलयंकृत्वोपरिचतुरस्त्रंकृत्वातदग्राणिसंवर्ध्यतत्रत्रिशूलानिकृत्वा-त्रिशूलेषुक्रोमिति वज्रेषुहसौमिति विलिख्यतन्माला मन्त्रेणवक्ष्यमाणेनंसंवेष्ट्य-तत्पुनर्वलयत्रयेणवेष्टयेत् ।।४८-५०।।

Naukā: 46-47. He explains the Mantra. The devotee is to draw three spiral lines in the shape of a tail. In the middle thereof he writes the name of the intended victim and encircles it with a number of "Ām". Beyond that he writes "Hum" in the eight petals.

Naukā: 48-50. Outside also he makes a circle and above it makes a square. The sides are extended and figures like trident are made therein within which he writes "Krom". In the Vajras (Inner cardinal edges) he writes Hsaum. All round, the Mālā Mantra (verses 54 et sq) is written and the whole figure is enclosed in three days.

नौका: नाभि: कस्तूरी ॥ त्यक्ताशडपवासी ॥५१-५३॥

Naukā: 51-53. Nabhi=Musk Tyaktāśa=one who fasts.

मालामंत्रमथोवक्ष्येप्रणवोवाग्धरिप्रिया ।
दीर्घत्रयान्वितामायापूर्वोक्तकूटपंचकम् ॥५४॥
तारोन मोहनुमतेप्रकटांतेपराक्रम ।
आक्रांतदिङ्मंडलतोयशोवीतिचतानिच ॥५५॥
धवलीकृतवर्णांतेज गत्रितयवज्रच ।
देहज्वलदग्निसूर्य्यकोट्यंतेतुसमप्रभ ॥५६॥
तनूरुहपदंरुद्रावतारपदमीरयेत् ।
लंकापुरीदहांतेनोदधिलंघनवर्णका ॥५७॥
दशग्रीवशिर:पश्चात्कृतांतकपदंतत: ।
सीताश्वा सनवाय्वतेसुतशब्दमुदीरयेत् ॥५८॥
अंजनागर्भसंभूतश्रीरामांतेतुलक्ष्मण: ।
नंदकांतेरकपिचसैन्य प्रकारवर्णका: ॥५९॥
सुग्रीवसख्यकांवर्णारणवालिनिबर्हण ।
कारणद्रोणपर्वांतेतोत्पाटनपदंव देत् ॥६०॥
अशोकवनवीत्यंतेदारणाक्षकुमारक: ।
च्छेदनांतेवनपदंरक्षाकरसमूहच ॥६१॥

विभंजनांतेब्रह्मास्त्रब्रह्मशक्तिग्रसेतिन ।
लक्ष्मणांतेशक्तिभेदनिवारणपदंपुनः ॥६२॥
विशल्यौषधिव र्णांतेसमानयनवर्णकाः ।
बालोदितांतेभान्वंतेमंडलग्रसनेतिच ॥६३॥
मेघनादेतिहोमांतेविध्वंसनपदं वदेत् ।
इन्द्रजिद्वधारांतेणसीतारक्षकेतिच ॥६४॥
राक्षसीसंघवर्णांतेविदारणचकुंभच ।
कर्णादिवधशब्दांतेपरायणपदंवदेत् ॥६५॥
श्रीरामभक्तिश ब्दांतेतत्परेतिसमुद्रच ।
व्योमद्रुमलंघनेतिमहासामर्थ्यमेतिच ॥६६॥
हा तेजःपुंजवीत्यंतेराजमानप दंपुनः ।
स्वामिवचनसंपादितार्जुनांतेचसंयुग ॥६७॥
सहायांतेकुमारेतिब्रह्मचारिन्पदंवदेत् ।
गंभीर शब्दोऽत्रिर्वायुर्दक्षिणाशापदंपुनः ॥६८॥
मार्तंडमेरुशब्दांतेपर्वतेतिपदंवदेत् ।
पीठिकार्चनशब्दां तेसकलेतिपदंपुनः ॥६९॥
मंत्रागमाचार्य्यममसर्वग्रहविनाशन ।
सर्वज्वरोच्चाटनेतिसर्वविषविनाशन ॥७०॥
सर्वापत्तिनिवारणसर्वदुष्टेतिसंपठेत् ।
निबर्हणपदंसर्वव्याघ्रादिभयतत्परम् ॥७१॥
विना रणंसर्वशत्रुच्छेदनेतिपदंमम ।
परस्यचत्रिभुवनपुंस्त्रीनपुंसककात्मकम् ॥७२॥
सर्वजीवपदंपश्चाज्जातंवशय युग्मकम् ।
ममाशाकारकंपश्चात्संपादयपदद्वयम् ॥७३॥
नानानामपदंधेयान्सर्वान्राज्ञःससंपठेत् ।
परिवारान्ममेत्यंतेसेवकान्कुरुयुग्मकम् ॥७४॥

सर्वशस्त्रास्त्रवीत्यंते षाणिविध्वंसयद्वयम् ।
मायादीर्घ त्रयोपेताहात्रयंचैहियुग्मकम् ॥७५॥
विलोमपंचकूटानिसर्वशत्रून्हनद्वयम् ।
परदांतेलानिपरसैन्या निक्षोभयद्वयम् ॥७६॥
ममसर्वकाय्जातंसाधयद्वितयंततः ।
सर्वदुष्टदुर्जनांतेमुखानिकीलयद्वयम् ॥७७॥
घेत्रयंहात्रयंवर्मत्रित यफट्त्रयंततः ।
वह्निप्रियांतोमंत्रोयंमालासंज्ञोखिलेष्टदः ॥७८॥

54-78. The *Mālāmantra* of Hanumān. This is of 588 syllables. (The Mantra is given in the commentary in full. The meanings of the different names are given here).

Om obeisance to Hanumān. O deity whose exploits are manifest, who traversed all the quorters, who had brightened the three worlds by your enveloping renown, of adamantine body, whose bodily haris have the lustre of the blazing fire and crores of suns, the incarnation of Rudra, one who burnt the city of Laṅkā, one who crossed the ocean, one who brought headache unto the ten headed Rāvaṇa, the comforter of Śītā, the son of Wind god, one born of the womb of Añjanā, the delighter of Śrī Rāma and Lakśmaṇa, a rampart unto the monkey host, one who brought about the friendship of Sugrīva, the cause of the destruction of Vālī, one who uprooted the Droṇa mountain, the destroyer of Aśoka grove, one who slew Akṣ akumāra, the destroyer of all the guards of the grove, one who could grasp and curb the Brahmāstra and Brahmaśakti, one who brought the medicinal herbs capable of healing the wounds of Lakṣmana due to the javelin prick, one who swallowed the disc of the rising sun even as a child, one who spoiled the Homa of Meghanāda, the cause of the death of Indrajit, one who attacked the group of demonesses who guarded Sītā, one who is engrossed in the devotion to Śrī Rāma who was eager to kill Kumbhakarṇa etc., one who had the great skill to jump over the tress, seas and the sky, one who shone with a great deal of splendour, one who went to the help of Arjuna in the battle at the behest of his lord and master, a life long celebate, one whose rorar is profound, a sun unto the southern quarter, one who worshipped mountain Meru as the pedestal, a preceptor of all the Mantras and Āgamas, the destroyer of all evil planets adverse to me, one who drives away all fever, the destroyer of all poisons, one who removes all dangers, the annihilator of all wicked people, one who removes the fear from the beasts of prey such as the tiger etc., the suppressor of all enemies, fascinate fascinate, all living beings whether males, female or neither belonging to me and to my enemy, get together, get together persons acting at my behest, make make all the officers and staff of the king, of different names, my servants, destroy destroy all the weapons and missiles and poisons, kill kill all the enmies, stir up the partisans and armies of the enemies, accomplish, accomplish all my tasks, nail up nail up the mouths of all wicked and evil minded persons.

नौका: मालामन्त्रमाह ।। प्रणवइति ।। वाक्ऐं ।। हरिप्रियाश्रीं ।। मायादीर्घत्रयान्विता ह्रांह्रींह्रूं ।। पूर्वोक्तंमूलमंत्रस्थम् ।।५४-६७।।

Naukā: 54-67. He explains the Mālā Mantra

Vāk = Aim

Haripriyā = Śrīm

Māyā with three long vowels – Hrām, Hrīm, Hrūm.

The five Kūṭas are in the Mūla Mantra mentioned before

Vāyu = Ya

The other things – form itself.

अष्टाशीत्युत्तरा:पंचशतवर्णामनो:स्मृता: ।
महोपद्रवसंपातेस्मृतोयंदु:खनाशन: ॥७९॥

79. It is to be remembered that there are five hundred and eighty eight syllables in this Mantra. When confronted by great calamities this Mantra should be recollected and it destroys misery.

नौका: अत्रि:द: ॥ वायु:य: स्वस्वरूपमनयत् ॥६८-७९॥

Naukā: 68-79. The Mālā Mantra as evolved in the 24 verses is as follows :

"Om Aim Śrīm Hrām Hrīm Hrūm Hsphrem Khphrem Hsraum Hskhphrem Hsaum Om Namo Hanumate Prakaṭa Parākrama Ākrāntadiṅmaṇḍala Yaśovitānadhavalīkṛta Jagattritaya Vajradeha Jvaladagni Sūryakoṭisamaprabha Tanūruha Rudrāvatāra Laṅkāpurī Dahanodadhilaṅ- ghanadaśagrīva Śiraḥkṛtātaṅka Sītāśvāsanavāyu-sutāñjanāgarbhasambhūta Śrī Rāmalakṣmaṇānandakara Kapi Sainyaprākāra Sugrīva Sakhya Kāraṇa Vālinibarhaṇakāraṇa Droṇaparvatotpāṭanāśoka Vanavidāraṇā Kṣa Kumāra Kacchedana Vanarakṣākarasamūha Vibhañjana Brahmāstra Brahmaśaktigrasana Lakṣmaṇaśaktibhedanivāraṇa Viśalyauṣadhisamānayana Bālodita Bhānumaṇḍala Grasana Meghanāda Homa Vidhvaṁsana Indrajidvadhakāraṇa Sītārakṣaka Rākṣasī Saṅgha Vidāraṇa Kumbhakar- ṇādivadhaparāyaṇa Śrī Rāma Bhaktitatpara Samudra Vyomadrumalaṅghana Mahāsāmarthya Mahātejaḥ Puñjavirājamāna Svāmivacana Saṁpāditārjuna Saṁyuga- sahāya Kumāra Brahmacārin Gambhīra Śabdodaya Dakṣiṇāśāmārtaṇḍa Meruparvata Pīṭhikārcana Sakalamantrā- gamācārya Mama Sarvagrahavināśana Sarvajvaroccāṭana Sarvaviṣavināśana Sarvāpattinivāraṇa Sarvaduṣṭanibarhaṇa Sarvavyāghrādibhayanivāraṇa Sarvasatrucchedana mama Parasyacatribhuvanapumstrī Napuṁsakātmaka Sarvajī- vajātam Vaśayavaśaya Mamājñākārakam Sampādaya Sampādaya Nānānāmadheyān Sarvān Rājñaḥ Saparivārān Mama Sevakān Kuru Kuru Sarvaśastrāstraviṣāṇī Vidhvaṁsaya Vidhvaṁsaya Hrām Hrīm Hīm (3 times) Ehyehi Hsaum Hskhphrem Hsraum Khphrem Hsphrem Sarvaśatrūn Hana Hana Paradalāni Parasainyāni Kśobhaya Kṣobhaya Mama Sarva Kārya Jātam Sādhaya Sādhaya Sarva Duṣṭa Durjana

Mukhāni Kīlaya Kilaya Ghe Ghe Ghe Hā Hā Hā Hum Hum Hum Phaṭ Phaṭ Phaṭ Svāhā" .

This Mālā Mantra is of 588 syllables.

द्वादशार्णांतिमान्वर्णान्षट्त्यक्त्वैकंतथादिमम् ।
पंचकू टात्मकोमंत्रोनिखिलाभीष्टसाधकः ॥८०॥

80. The Mantra consisting of only the five Kūṭas after dropping the last six syllables as well as the first Kūṭa, is the accomplisher of all cherished desires.

मुनीरामोथगायत्रीछन्दोदेवःकपीश्वरः ।
पंचबीजैःसमस्तेनषडंगंमुनिभिः स्मृतम् ॥८१॥
रामदूतो लक्ष्मणांतेप्राणदातांजनासुतः ।
सीताशोकविनाशोथलंकाप्रासादभंजनः ॥८२॥
हनूमदाद्याः पंचैतेबी जाद्याङेसमन्विताः ।
षडंगमंत्राः संदिष्टाध्यानपूजादिपूर्ववत् ॥८३॥

81-83. The sage of this Mantra is Rāma, the metre is Gāyatrī and the deity is the lord of the monkeys.

The Ṣaḍaṅga Nyāsa is to be performed by means of the five Bījas severally and collectively for the sixth. The word Hanumān in the beginning and the words Rāma Dūta (Messenger of Rāma), Lakṣmaṇā Prāṇadātā (one who gave life to Lakṣmaṇa), Añjanāsutā (son of Añjanā), Sītāśokavināśa (the destroyer of the sorrow of Sītā) and Laṅkā Prāsāda Bhaūjana (one who demolished the palaces in Laṅkā) should also be used in the dative case along with the Bījas referred to.

The procedure of worship, mode of Dhyāna etc. as before.

नौकाः चतुर्विंशतिश्लोकैर्निष्पत्नोमालामंत्रो यथा–ओंऐंश्रींह्रांह्रींह्रूंह्रैंह्रूस्फ्रें–ह्रूस्त्रौंह्रूसूख्फ्रेंह्रूसौंओंनमोहनुमतेप्रकदृपराक्रमख्फ्रेंमआक्रांतदिडमंडलयशोवितान–धवलीकृतजगत्रितयवज्रदेहज्वलदग्निसूर्यकोटिसमप्रभतनूरुहरुद्रावतारालंकापुरीद–

हनोदधिलंघनदश ग्रीवशिरः कृतांतकसीताश्वासनवायुसुतांजनागर्भसंभूतश्रीराम-लक्ष्मणानंदकरकपिसैन्यप्राकारसुग्रीवसख्यकारणवालिनिबर्हणकारण द्रोणपर्व-तोत्पाटनाशोकवनविदारणाक्षकुमारकच्छेदनवनरक्षाकरसमूहविभंजनब्रह्मास्त्रब्रह्म-शक्तिग्रसनलक्ष्मणशक्तिभेदनिवारणबिशल्यौषधिसमानयनबालोदितभानुमंडल-ग्रसनमेघनादहोमविध्वंसनइंद्रजिद्वधकारणसीतारक्षकराक्षसींसघविदारणकुंभकर्णा-दिवधपरायण श्रीरामभक्तितत्परसमुद्रव्योमद्रुमलंघन महासामर्थ्य-महातेजःपुजवीराजमानस्वामिबचनसंपादितार्जुनसंयुगसहायकुमार ब्रह्मचारिन्गंभी रशब्दोदयदक्षिणाशामार्तंडमेरुपर्वतपीठिकार्चनसकलमंत्रागमाचार्यममसर्वग्रहविनाशन-सर्वज्वरोच्चाटनसर्वविषविनाशनसर्वापत्तिनिवांरणसर्वदुष्टनिबर्हणसर्वव्याघ्रादिभय-निवारणसवशत्रुच्छेदनममपरस्यचत्रिभुवनंपुसकात्मकसर्वजीवजातंवशय २ममाज्ञा-कारकंसंपाद य २ नानानामधेयान्सर्वात्राज्ञः सपरिवारान्ममसेवकान्कुरु २ सर्वशस्त्रास्त्रविषाणिविध्वंसय२ह्रांह्रींहूं ह्रां३ एह्येहिह्सौंह्स्ख्फ्रहस्फ्रेहौंसर्वशत्रून्हन २ परदलानिपरसैन्यानिक्षोभय २ ममसर्वकार्यजातंसाधय २ सर्वदुष्टदुर्जनमुखानिकीलय २ घे ३ हा ३ हुं ३ फटू ३ स्वाहा मालांमंत्रोयमष्टाशीत्यधिकपंचशतवर्णः (५८८) ।। मंत्रांतरमाह ।। द्वादशेति ।। द्वादशाक्षरस्यांतिमान्षड्वर्णान् हनुमतेनम इति।। प्रथममेकंहौमितित्यक्त्वाशेषः पंचार्णोमंत्रः-ह्स्फ्रेख्फेंह्स्रौंहरख्फ्रेंह्सौमिति ।।८०-८१।।

नौकाः षडंगमाह ।। रामदूतइति ।। हनुम दाद्याश्चतुर्थ्यंताबीजपूर्वाः षडंगमंत्राः ।। यथा-हस्फ्रेंहनुमतेंहृत् ।। ख्फ्रेंरामभक्तायशिरः ।। हस्रौलक्ष्मणप्राणदात्रेशिखेत्यादि० ।।८२।।

नौकाः पूर्ववद्द्वादशवर्णवत् ।।८३।।

Naukā: 80-81. He explains another Mantra. The last six syllables of 12 syllabled Mantra - Hanumate Namaḥ. The first Bīja is Haum. Leaving these two the remaining part constitutes the Pañcakūṭa Mantra *i.e.* Hsphrem, Khphrem, Hsraum, Hskhphrem, Hsaum

Naukā: 82. He explains Ṣaḍaṅga Nyāsa. The word Hanumān etc. should be used in the dative. The respective Bīja also should be used in the beginning. This will be the Mantra for Ṣaḍaṅga Nyāsa e.g.

Hsphrem hanumate obeisance to the heart

Khphrem Rāmadūtāya Svāhā unto the head

Hsraum Lakṣmaṇaprāṇadātre Vaṣaṭ unto the tuft etc.

Naukā: 83. As before *i.e.* as in the case of 12 syllabled one.

तारोवाक्कमलामायादीर्घत्रयसमन्विता: ।
पंचकूटानिमंत्रोयंरुद्राणोंऽभीष्टसिद्धिद: ॥८४॥
अर्चनात्पू र्ववच्चास्यपरोमंत्रोभिधीयते ।
हृदयंभगवान्ङेतंआंजनेयमहाबलौ ॥८५॥
तद्वद्वह्निप्रियांतोयंमनुरष्टाद शाक्षर: ।
मुनिरीश्वरएवास्यानुष्टुपूछंद: समीरितम् ॥८६॥
हनूमान्देवताबीजंहुंशक्तिर्वह्निवल्लभा ।
आंजनेयोरुद्रमूर्तिर्वायुपुत्रस्तथैवच ॥८७॥
अग्निगर्भोरामदूतोब्रह्मास्त्रविनिवारण: ।
एतैर्ङेंते: षडंगा निकृत्वाध्यायेत्कपीश्वरम् ॥८८॥

84-88. Another eleven syllabled Mantra of Hanumān is as follows :

"Om Aim Śrīm Hrām Hrīm Hrūm Hsphrem Khphrem Hsraum Hskhphrem Hsaum"

It bestows desired supernatural powers. The mode of worship of this Mantra is as before.

Now another Mantra is being explained. It is an eighteen syllabed Mantra :

"Namo Bhagavate Āñjaneyāya Mahābalāya Svāhā"

The sage of this Mantra is Īśvara himself. The metre is Anuṣṭup. The deity is Hanumān. Hum is the Bīja and Svāhā is Śakti.

The Ṣaḍaṅga Nyāsa is by means of the dative forms of Āñjaneya (Son of Āñjanā), Rudramūrti (Form of Rudra), Vāyuputra (Son of Wind god), Agnigarbha (Born of the womb of Agni), Rāmadūta (Messenger of Rāma), and Brahmāstra Nivārana (One who can ward off Brahmā missile). After the Ṣaḍaṅga the devotee shall meditate on the lord of the monkeys.

नौका: मंत्रांतरमाह ।। तारइति ।। तार ॐ ।। वाक्ऐं ।। कमलाश्रीं ।। माया-दीर्घत्रयाद्या ह्रांह्रींहूं ।। पंचकूटानिचइदानीमुक्तानि ।। रुद्रार्णएकाद शाक्षर: ।।८४।।

Naukā: 84. he explains another Mantra

Tāra=Om

Vāk=Aim

Kamalā=Śrīm

Māyā with three long vowels–Hrām, Hrīm Hrūm

"Namo Bhagavate Āñjaneyāya Mahābalāya Svāhā".

नौका: मंत्रांतरमाह ।। हृदयमिति ।। तद्वत् ।। ह्रंतोनमोभगवतआंजनेयाय-महाबलायस्वाहेति ।। षडंगमाह ।। आंजनेयइति ।। आंजनेयायहृत् ।। रुद्रमूर्तयेशिरइत्यादि० ।।८५-८८।।

Naukā: 85-88. He explains Ṣaḍaṅga

Āñjaneyāya obeisance to the heart

Rudramūrtaye Svāhā unto the head

दहनतप्तसुवर्णसमप्रभंभयहरंहृदयेविहितांजलितम् ।
श्रवणकुंडल शोभिमुखांबुजंनमतवानरराजमिहाद्भुतम् ।।८९।।

89. *Dhyāna Verse.* Bow down ye all to the wonderful king of monkeys whose lustre is like that of molten gold, who removes fear, who has kept his palms joined against his heart and whose lotus like face shines with earrings.

नौका: ध्यानमाह ।। दहनेति ।।८९।।

Naukā: 89. He explains Dhyāna.

अयुतंप्रजपेन्मंत्रंदशांशंजुहुयात्तिलै: ।
वैष्णवेपूज येत्पीठेपूर्ववत्कपिनायकम् ।।९०।।

90. He shall repeat the mantra ten thousand times and perform thousand Homas with gingelly seeds. As before

the devotee shal worship the lord of the monkeys in the Vaiṣṇava pedestal [verses 10-13].

जितेंद्रियोनक्तभोजीप्रत्यहंसाष्टकंशतम् ।
जपित्वाक्षुद्ररोगेश्यो मुच्यतेदिवसत्रयात् ॥९१॥

91. If the devotee abstains from sensual pleasures and takes food onlyh at night and repeats the Mantra hundred and eight times every day he gets relief from all minor ailments in three days.

नौका: प्रयोगानाह ॥ जितेन्द्रि यइति ॥९१-९७॥

Naukā: 91-97. He explains various rites.

भूतप्रेतपिशाचादिनाशायैवंसमाचरेत् ।
महारोगनीवृत्त्यैतुसहस्त्रंप्रत्यहंजपेत् ॥९२॥

92. For the purpose of the destruction of evil spirits, ghosts, genii etc. the same rite has to be performed. For the purpose of relief from major ailments he shall repeat the Mantra thousand times every day.

यताशनोऽयुतं नित्यंजपन्ध्यायन्कपीश्वरम् ।
राक्षसौघंविनिघ्नंतमचिराज्जयतिद्विषम् ॥९३॥

93. They devotee shall exercise restriction in diet and repeat the Mantra ten thousand times every day meditating on the lord of the monkeys slaying the hosts of Rākṣasa. Erelong he shall defeat his enemy.

सुग्रीवेणसमंरामंसं दधानंस्मरन्कपिम् ।
प्रजप्यायुतमेतस्यसंधिंकुर्य्याद्विरुद्धयोः ॥९४॥

94. The devotee shall meditate on the monkey effecting the alliance between Rāma and Sugrīva and repeat the Mantra ten thousand times. He will become competent to bring together two mutually opposing parties.

लंकांदहंतंतंध्यायन्नयुतंप्रजपे न्मनुम् ।
शत्रूणांप्रदहेद्ग्रामानचिरादेवसाधकः ॥९५॥

95. The aspirant devotee shall meditate upon the lord of the monkeys burning Laṅkā and repeat the Mantra ten thousand times. Erelong he will be able to burn down the villages of his enemies.

प्रयाणसमयेध्यायन्हनूमंतंमनुंजपन् ।
योंया तिसोऽचिरात्स्वेष्टंसाधयित्वागृहंव्रजेत् ॥९६॥

96. When starting on a journey the devotee shall meditate on Hanumān and repeat the Mantra. Ere long he shall accomplish his desired objective and return home.

यः कपीशंसदागेहेपूजयेज्जपतत्परः ।
आयुर्लक्ष्म्यौप्र वर्द्धेतेतस्यनश्यंत्युपद्रवाः ॥९७॥

97. If a devotee is devoutly engaged in repeating the Mantra and worships the lord of monkeys always in his house his life and prosperity increase and calamities become extinct.

शार्दूलतस्करादिश्योरक्षेन्मनुरयंस्मृतः ।
प्रस्वापकालेचौरेश्योदुष्ट स्वप्नादपिध्रुवम् ॥९८॥

98. This Mantra, scrupulously remembered, shall protect the devotee from tigers, thieves etc. If it is recollected at the time of going to bed it shall save him from robbers and ward off evil dreams certainly.

नौकाः ध्रुवंओंकारः ॥९८॥

Naukā: 98. Dhruva=Om.

पवनद्वितयंसद्योजातयुक्तंहनूपदम् ।
महाकालः शशांकाढ्यः कामिकाफल फःक्रिया ॥९९॥
सनेत्राणांतमीनोगसात्वतोगितआयुरा ।
षलोहितंरुडाहेतिवेदनेत्राक्षरोमनुः ॥१००॥

99-100. The following 24 syllabled Mantra is an antidote for the ailment of enlargement of the spleen. It is as follows :

"Om Yo Yo Hanūmanta Phalaphalita Dhaga Dhagita Āyurāṣaparudāha".

नौका: उदररोगनाशकमंत्रमाह ।। पवनेति ।। सद्योजातओंकारस्त द्युतपवनद्वययोयो ।। हनुस्वरूपं ।। शशांकाढयोमहाकाल: सबिंदुर्म: मं ।। कामिका न: ।। फलस्वरूपान्तेसनेप्राक्रिया इयु तोल: लि ।। णांतस्त: ।। मीनोध: ।। गस्वरूपं ।। सात्वतोध: ।। गितआयुरापस्वरूपं ।। लोहितंप: ।। रुडाहस्वरूपं वेदनेत्राक्षर: चतुर्विंशत्यर्ण: ।। यथा-ओंयोयोहनुमंतफलितधगधगित: आयुराषपरुडाहेति ।।९९-१००।।

Naukā: 99-100. He explains the Mantra destructive of spleen

Sadyojāta = O

Pavanadvayam – Ya – Ya together with O – Yo Yo

Hanu – form itself

Śaśāṅkāḍhya Mahākāla = Ma + M = Mam

Kāmikā = Ta

Sanetrākriyā = Li

Ṇānta = Ta

Mīna = Dha

Ga – form itself

Sāttvata = Dha

Gita Āyurāṣa – form itself

Lohita = Pa

Rudāha – form itself

Veda Netrākṣara = Having 24 syllables e.g.

"Om Yo Yo Hanumanta Phala Phalita Dhaga Dhagita Āyurāṣ a Paruḍāha".

प्लीहरोगहरश्चास्यमुन्याद्यंपूर्ववन्मतम् ।
प्लीहयुक्तोदरेस्थाप्यंनागवल्लीदलंशुभम् ।।१०१।।

तदुपर्य्यष्ट गुणितंवस्त्रमाच्छादयेत्ततः ।
वंशजंशकलंतस्योपरिमुंचेत्कपिंस्मरन् ॥१०२॥
आरण्यप्रस्तरोत्पन्नेवह्नौ यष्टिंप्रतापयेत् ।
बदरीतरुसंभूतांमंत्रेणानेनसप्तशः ॥१०३॥
तयासंताडयेद्वंशंशकलंजठरस्थितम् ।
सप्त कृत्वःप्लीहरोगोनश्यत्येवनृणांक्षणात् ॥१०४॥

101-104. The sage etc. of the Mantra, as before. An auspicious beteal leaf is to be placed on the belly with enlarged spleen. A cloth folded eight times shall be used to cover it. The devotee shall place a piece of bamboo on it meditating on Hanumān.

Fire is to be kindled by rubbing two pieces of rock from the forest. A stick of Badarī branch shall be warmed seven times over that fire. Repeating this Mantra the devotee shall hit the bamboo piece with this Badarī stick seven times. The ailment of enlarged spleen shall get healed instantaneously.

नौका: प्लीहरोग: उदररोग: ॥ तन्नाशकप्रयोगमाह ॥ प्लीहेति ॥१०१॥

नौका: आरण्यप्रस्तरोत्पन्नेवनपाषाणान्निष्कासितेग्नौंबदर्युत्थाय ष्टिंसप्तधामूल-मंत्रेणतापयेत् ॥१०३॥

नौका: तयोदरस्थितेवंशखंडेताडितेरोगोनश्यति ॥१०४॥

Naukā: 101. Plīharoga—Enlargement of the spleen. He explains rite destructie thereof.

Naukā: 103. In the fire brought about from the piece of rock in the forest. The devotee shall warm seven times the stick from the branch of Badarī in the said fire.

Naukā: 104. If the piece of bamboo placed on the belly is hit with that stick the ailment gets healed.

पुच्छाकारेसुवसनेलेखिन्याकोकिलोत्थया ।
अष्टंगधैर्लि खेद्रूपंकपिराजस्यसुंदरम् ॥१०५॥

तन्मध्येष्टादशार्णंतुशत्रुनामयुतलिखेत् ।
तेनमंत्राभिजप्तेनशिरोब द्धेनभूमिपः ॥१०६॥
जयत्यरिगणंसर्वंदर्शनादेवनिश्चितम् ।
युद्धेजिगीषुर्नृपतिः पूर्वोक्तंलेखयेद्ध्वजे ॥१०७॥

105-107. Take an excellent cloth cut in the form of a tail. The feather of the cuckoo is used as stylus and the beautiful picture of the lord of the monkeys is drawn with the eight fragrant substances as material for writing. In the middle the devotee shall write the 18 syllabled Mantra along with the name of the enemy.

The cloth shall be inspired with the Mantra. The king shall wear that cloth as a turban. Certainly at the very sight of that king the enemies shall be defeated.

A king desirous of being victorious in battle shall get the Mantra written on his banner along with the picture of Hanumān and the inscription of the name of the enemy. The banner shall be held aloft at the time of an eclipse from the beginning till the end and the Mātṛkā syllables shall be repeated continuously. Homas shall be performed one tenth of that number with mustard mixed with gingelly seeds from the beginning till the close of the eclipse. If the enemies see that banner on the elephant they shall flee erelong.

Hanumad Yantra

ध्वजमादायोपरागेसंस्पर्शान्मोक्षणावधि ।
मातृकांजापयेत्पश्चाद्दशांशेनचहावयेत् ॥१०८॥
सर्षपैस्तिलसंमिश्रैःसंस्पर्शान्मोक्षणावधि ।
गजस्थंतंध्वजंदृष्ट्वापलायंतेऽरयोऽचिरात् ॥१०९॥
अथोहनुमतोयंत्रंवक्ष्येरक्षाविधायकम् ।
लिखेदष्टदलंपद्मंसाध्याख्यायुतकर्णिकम् ॥११०॥

110. I shall now explain the Yantra of Hanumān which brings about safety. The devotee shall make an eight petalled lotus with the pericarp containing the name of the intended victim.

नौका: प्रयोगांतरमाह ॥ पुच्छेति ॥ पुच्छाकारेव स्त्रेकोकिलापिच्छलेखिन्याऽष्टगंधैर्हनुमज्जपंकृत्वातदुदरेऽष्टादशार्णंविलिख्याधिमंत्रितेनशिरोबद्धेनतेनारीञ्जयति ॥१०५-१०९॥

नौका: यंत्रमाह ॥ लिखेदिति ॥११०॥

Naukā: 105-109. He explains another rite. In the cloth of the shape of the tail – with the stylus made of the feather of the cuckoo Making the form of Hanumān with eight fragrant substances – The eighteen syllabled Mantra must be written in the belly of the image. The cloth should be inspired with the Mantra and the head is tied with it. Thereby the devotee can defeat the enemies.

Naukā: 110. He explains the mystic diagram.

दलेष्वष्टार्णमा लिख्यमालामंत्रेणवेष्टयेत् ।
तद्बहिर्मायियावेष्ट्यप्राणास्थापनामाचरेत् ॥१११॥

111. The eight syllabled Mantra shall be written in the petals and enveloped with the Mālā Mantra [garland of Mantras verses 116 et sq]. This shall then be covered externally by Hrīm (written many times). Then the rite of Prāṇasthāpana (instilling vital airs) shall be performed.

लिखितंस्वर्णलेखिन्या दलेभूर्जतरोः शुभे ।
रोचनाकुंकुमाश्यांतुवेष्टितंकनकादिभिः ॥११२॥
संपातसाधितंयंत्रंभुजेवामूर्ध्नि धारयेत् ।
रणेजवमवाप्नोतिव्यवहारेदुरोदरे ॥११३॥
ग्रहैर्विघ्नैर्विषैः शस्त्रैश्चौरैर्नैवाभिभूयते ।
रोगा न्सर्वानपाकृत्य चिरंजीवतिभाग्यवान् ॥११४॥

112-114. With a gold stylus this mystic diagram is to

be written in the auspicous leaf of Bhūrja tree using Rocana and saffron as materials for writing. It shall then be sanctified by the residue of Homa ghee. Then the entire piece shall be enclosed in an amulet of gold or other metals. This amulet is to be worn on the head or on the arm. The devotee shall become victorious in battle, win in law siuts and gaming table, he is never tormented by adverse planets, obstacles, poisons substances, weapons or thieves. He shall get rid of all ailments and be fortunate. He shall live a long life.

नौका: अष्टार्णमालामंत्रौवक्ष्यमाणौ ।।१११-११२।।

नौका: दुरोदरेद्यूते ।।११३।। ।।११४।।

Naukā: 111-112. The eight syllabled Mantra and the Mālā Mantra are being explained presently.

Naukā: 113-114. Durodare–in the game of dice.

वियदग्नियुतंदीर्घषट्काद्यंतारसंपुटम् ।
अष्टार्णो मंत्रआख्यातोमालामंत्रोऽकथ्यते ।।११५।।

115. The eight syllabled Mantra is as follows :
"Om Hrām Hrīm Hrūm Hraim Hraum Hraḥ Om"
Now the Mālā Mantra is being mentioned.

नौका: अष्टा र्णमाह ।। वियदिति ।। वियत्ह: ।। अग्नीर: ।। यथा-ओंह्रांह्राह्हंह्रंह्रि: ओंइत्याष्टार्ण: ।।११५।।

Naukā: 115. He explains the 8 syllabled Mantra–

Agni=Ra e.g.

"Om Hrām Hrīm Hrūm Hraim Hraum Hraḥ Om"

This is the eight syllabled one.

वज्रकायवज्रतुंडकपिलेत्यथपिंगला ।
ऊद्ध्र्वकेशमहाव र्णबलरक्तमुखेतिच ।।११६।।

तडिज्जिह्वमहारौद्रदंष्ट्रोत्कटकहद्वयम् ।
करालिनेमहादृढप्रहारिन्निति वर्णका: ॥११७॥
लंकेश्वरब धायांतेमहासेतुपदंततः ।
बंधांतेचमहाशैलप्रवाहगगनेचर ॥११८॥
ऐह्येहिभगवंन्नतेमहाबलपराक्रम ।
भैरवाज्ञापयैह्येहिमहारौद्रपदंपुनः ॥११९॥
दीर्घपुच्छेनवर्णांतिवेष्टयांतेतुवैरिणम् ।
भंजयद्वितयंहुफट्प्र णवादिसमीरितः ॥१२०॥
बाणनेत्रेंदुवर्णोयंमालामंत्रोखिलेष्टदः ।
युद्धेजतोजयंदद्याव्द्याधौव्याधि विनाशनः ॥१२१॥
अष्टार्णमालामन्वोस्तुमुन्याद्यर्च्चातुपूर्ववत् ।
भूरिणाकिमिहोक्तेनसर्वंदद्यात्कपीश्वरः ॥१२२॥

116-122. The Hundred and twenty-five syllables Mālā Mantrā is as follows :

"Om Vajrakāya Vajratuṇḍa Kapila Piṅgala Ūrdhvakeśa Mahābala Raktamukha Taḍijjihva Mahāraudra Daṁṣṭrotkaṭ aka Ha Ha Karāline Mahādṛḍha Prahārin Laṅkeśvara Vadhāya Mahāsetubandha Mahāśaila Pravāha Gaganecara Ehyehi Bhagavan Mahābala Parākrama Bhairava Ājñāpaya Ehyehi Mahāraudra Dīrgha Pucchena Veṣṭaya Vairiṇam Bhañjaya Bhañjaya Hum Phaṭ"

It is the bestower of all desired objectives.

If it is repeated at the time of war it shall accord victory; during illness, it shall destroy the ailments.

The sage etc. and procedure of worship etc. as before.

Why tell a lot? The lord of monkeys shall give everything.

इति श्रीमंत्रमहोदधौहनुमन्मंत्रकथनंनामत्रयोदशस्तरंगः ॥१३॥

नौकाः मालामंत्रमाह ।। वज्रेति यथा-ओंवज्र कायवज्रतुडकपिलापिंगल-ऊर्ध्वकेशमहाबलरक्तमुखतडिज्जिह्वमहारौद्रद्रंष्टोत्कटकहहकरालिनेमहादृढप्रहारिन्ल-कश्वरबधांयामहासेतुबंध महाशैलप्रवाहगगनेचरएह्येहिभग- वन्महाबलपराक्रम-भैरवापयज्ञापय एह्येहिमांहारौद्रदीर्घपुच्छेनवेष्टयवैरिणंभंजय २ हुंफट् ।।११६-१२०।।

नौकाः बाणनेत्रेंदुवर्णः पंचविंशत्युत्तरशतार्णः ।।१२१।।

नौकाः अष्टार्णमालामंत्रौस्वतंत्राविति सूचयन्नाह अष्टार्णेति ।।१२२।।

Naukā: 116-120. He explains the Mālā Mantra. The meaning of the Mālā Mantra :

O deity of adamantine body, of adamantine noose, of brown and tawny complexion, having the hair standing upright, of great strenth, of red face, having the tongue resembling lightning, extremely fierce of terrible curved fangs, terrible one, striking hard, one who makes the great bridge for the destruction of the lord of Laṅka, moving about like a great mountain, walking in the sky, come, come, O great lord of great strength and exploit, Terrifying one, command, come, come, of extremely terrible form, encircle with you long tail, strike the enemy strike Hum Phaṭ.

Naukā: 121. Bānanetrenduvarṇa–having hundred and twentyfive syllables.

Naukā: 122. The eight syllabled and the Mālā Mantra are independent of one another is indicated.

इतिश्रीमंत्रमहोदधिव्याख्यायांनौकायांत्रयोदशस्तरगः ।।१३।।

Notes

The theme of this book is the worship of Hanumān which is of comparatively recent origin, say 13th and 14th centuries,, according to some established Indologists. The political instability and utter confusion due to wars and skirmishes seems to have instilled the desire for having a deity of starner stuff for fighting with the enemies.

10 et sq. The procedure for the worship of the pedestal.

The Mystic diagram (See Plate 31) has a circular pericarp, then eight petalled lotus and then Bhūpura (square).

The worship begins with mental obeisance. The deity is meditated upon (Verse 8) and the preliminary rites are gone through.

In the middle

Om obeisance to Ādhāra Śakti

" " " Prakṛti

" " " Kūrma

" " " Ananta

" " " Pṛthvī

" " " the Milk Ocean

" " " Śveta Dvīpa

" " " Maṇimaṇḍapa

" " " Kalpavṛkṣa

" " " Maṇivedikā

" " " Gemstudded throne

Then in the quarters

Om obeisance to Dharma – south-east

„ „ „ Jñāna – south-west

„ „ „ Vairāgya – north-west

„ „ „ Aiśvarya – north-east

„ „ „ Adharma – east

„ „ „ Ajñāna – south

„ „ „ Avairāgya-west

„ „ „ Anaiśvarya – north

Again in the middle

Om obeisance to Ananta to Padma

Om Am „ „ Solar disc of 12 Kalās

Om Um „ „ Lunar disc of 16 Kalās

Om Ram „ „ Fiery disc of 10 Kalās

Om Sam „ „ Sattva

Om Ram „ „ Rajas

Om Tam „ „ Tamas

Om Ām „ „ Ātman

Om Am „ „ Antarātman

Om Pam „ „ Paramātman

Om Hrīm „ „ Jñānātman

Then in the filaments beginning with the east –

Om obeisance to Vimalā

„ „ „ Utkarṣiṇī

„ „ „ Jñāna

„ „ „ Kriyā

„ „ „ Yoga

„ „ „ Prahvī

„ „ „ Satyā

„ „ „ Īśānā

(middle) Om obeisance to Anugrahā

Dhyāna, Āvāhana and other ancillary rites are then performed.

Mantras to Viṣṇu, Narasiṁha, Gopāla and Garuḍa

अथ वक्ष्येमहाविष्णो र्मंत्रान्सर्वार्थसाधकान् ।

ब्रह्माद्यायानुपास्याथससृजुर्विविधाः प्रजाः ॥१॥

1. Now I shall explin the Mantras of Mahāviṣṇu that can enable us to achieve all objects of desires Brahmā and others made use of them for worship and created different kinds of people.

नौकाः विष्णुमंत्रान्वक्तुंप्रतिजानीते ॥ अथेति ॥१॥

Naukā: 1. He proclaims his intention to explain Viṣṇu Mantras.

मेरुःकृशानुसंयुक्तोऽनुग्रहें दुसमन्वितः ।

एकाक्षरोनरहरेर्मंत्रः कल्पद्रुमोनृणाम् ॥२॥

त्र्यक्षरः संपुटःप्रोक्तोमाययाप्रणेवनच ।

ऋषिरत्रिश्चगायत्रीछंदोदेवानृकेसरी ॥३॥

षड्दीर्घयुक्तबी जेनषडंगानिसमाचरेत् ।

त्र्यर्णेमायापुटेनैवतारसंपुटितेनवा ॥४॥

2-4. The single syllabled Mantra of Narahari is Kṣ raum. It is the wish yielding Kalpa tree for men. It becomes three syllabled when Hrīm or Om is used for Sampuṭa.

The sage for these Mantras is Atri and the metre is Gāyatrī. The deity is Nṛkesari (Narasimha).

The Bīja syllable with six long vowels is to be used for Ṣaḍaṅga Nyāsa for the three syallbled Mantra whether Māyā or Pranava is used for Sampuṭa.

नौका: मंत्रानाह ।। मेरुरिति ।। मेरु:क्ष: ।। कृशानूर: ।। अनुग्रहऔ ।। इंदुर्बिंदु: ।। तेनक्ष्रौं ।।२।।

नौका: मायाह्रीं ।। तत्संपुट: प्रणवसंपुटश्चेति द्वौत्र्यर्णौ ।।३-४।।

Naukā: 2. Meru=Kṣa Kṛśānu=Ra

Anugraha=Au Indu=M

Hence—Kṣraum.

Naukā: 3-4. Māyā=Hrīm. Sampuṭa with Hrīm as well as with Praṇava. Hence two Mantras with three syllables each.

तपनसोमहुताशनलोचनंघनविरा महिमांशुसमप्रभम् ।
अभयचक्रपिनाकवरान्करैर्दधतमिंदुधरंनृहरिंभजे ।।५।।

5. *Dhyāna Verse.* I worship Nṛhari who has three eyes with Sun, Moon and Fire, whose lustre is like that of the moon at the close of the days of cloud who holds the discus and the Pināka in the upper arms and Vara and Abhaya in the lower ones and who is adorened with the Moon.

नौका: ध्यानमाह ।। तपनेति ।। सूर्येद्वग्निनेत्रं ।। घनविराम: शरत्तत्रयोहिमांशुश्चंद्रस्तत्तुल्यकांति: घनसमानलमितिपाठेनीलकंठं ।। शशिसप्रभमितिपाठान्तरेशशिनासमानाप्रभायस्यतम् ।। ऊर्ध्वयोर्दक्षवामयोश्चक्र पिनाकौ ।। अध्स्थयोर्वराभये ।। इंदुधरंशशिशेखरम् ।।५।।

Naukā: 5. He explains the Dhyāna. The lord has the sun, moon and fire as his three eyes. Ghanavirāma=Autumn. The moon then. The lord has the lustre of the moon. There is a reading Ghanasamānagala meaning blue throated. In the reading Śaśi Saprabham it means having lustre similar to that of the moon. In the upper right and left hands (he holds) discus and Pināka bow. In the lower ones the gestures of boon and fear lessness. Indudharam=Moon crested.

लक्षमेकंजपेन्मंत्रंदशां शघृतपायसैः ।
जुहुयात्पूजयेत्पीठेविमलादिसमन्विते ॥६॥

6. The devotee shall repeat the Mantra a hundred thousand times and perform ten thousand Homas with ghee and milk pudding. He shall worship the deity in the pedestal having Vimalā etc. (as the Śaktis)

नौका: विमलादयउक्ता: ॥६॥

Naukā: 6. Vimalā and others have been mentioned.

केसरेष्वंगपूजास्याद्दिद्ल लेषुखगेश्वरम् ।
शंकरंशेषनागंचशतानंदंप्रपूजयेत् ॥७॥
श्रियंह्रियंधृतिंपुष्टिंकोणपत्रेषुसाधकः ।
द्वात्रिंशत्पत्रमध्येषु नृसिंहांस्तावतोर्चयेत् ॥८॥

7-8. In the filaments the six Aṅgas are to be worshipped. In the petals of the four quarters Khageśvara (Lord of Birds – Garuḍa), Śaṅkara, Śeṣanāga and Śatānanda are to be worshipped. The aspirant devotee then worships Śrī, Hrī, Dhṛti and Puṣṭi in the corner petals. He shall worship the 32 Narasiṁhas in the 32 petals.

नौका: शतानदंब्रह्माणम् ॥७॥

नौका: तावतोद्वात्रिंशत्सं ख्याकान् ॥८॥

Naukā: 7. Śatānandam = Brahmā.

Naukā: 8. Tāvataḥ = 32 in number.

कृष्णोरुद्रोमहाघोरोभीमोभीषणउज्वलः ।
करालोधिकरालश्चदैत्यांतोमधुसूदनः ॥९॥
रक्ताक्षः पिंगलाक्षश्चांजनसंज्ञस्त्रयोदशः ।
दीप्ततेजाः सुघोणश्चहनुर्वैषोडशः स्मृतः ॥१०॥

विश्वा क्षोराक्षसांतश्चविशालोधुम्रकेशवः ।
हयग्रीवोघनस्वरोमेघनादस्तथापरः ॥११॥
मेघवर्णःकुंभकर्णः कृतांतक इतीरितः ।
तीव्रतेजाअग्निवर्णोमहोग्रोविश्वभूषणः ॥१२॥
विघ्नक्षमोमहासेनः सिंहोद्वात्रिं शदीरिताः ।
इंद्रादीन्वज्रमुख्यांश्चपूजयेच्चतुरस्त्रके ॥१३॥

9-13. They are Kṛṣṇa, Rudra, Mahāghora, Bhīma, Bhīṣaṇa, Ujjvala, Karāla, Vikarāla, Daityānta, Madhusūdana, Raktākṣa, Piṅgalākṣa, Añjana, Dīptatejas, Sughoṇa, Suhanu, Viśvākṣa, Rākṣasānta, Viśala, Dhūmrakeśaka, Hayagrīva, Ghanasvara, Meghanāda, Meghavarṇa, Kumbhakarṇa, Kṛtāntaka, Tivratejas, Agnivarṇa, Mahogra, Viśvabhūṣaṇa, Vighnakṣama and Mahāsena. These are the 32 Simhas. In the square the devotee worships Indra and others as well as thunderbolt and other weapons.

नौकाः तानाह ॥९-१३॥

Naukā: 9-13. He enumerates them—Kṛṣṇa etc.

एवंसंसाधितोमंत्रःप्रयोगेषुक्षमोभवेत् ।
स हस्त्राष्टकसंख्यातैःशतपर्वात्रिकैस्तुयः ॥१४॥
जुहुयादुदकेतस्यसर्वेनश्यंत्युपद्रवाः ।
महोत्पातहरोप्ये षहोमः सर्वेष्टदोनृणाम् ॥१५॥

14-15. The Mantra perfected thus can be capable of being used in efficacious rites. If the devotee performs 1008 Homas in water with three knotted Dūrvā grass all his calamities perish. This Homa is desructive of great calamities and it bestows all desired objects to men.

संस्थाप्यविधिवत्कुंभंजपेदष्टसहस्त्रकम् ।
अभिषिंचेद्विषाक्रांतंवि षजार्तिनिवृत्तये ॥१६॥

16. For the purpose of removing the grief caused by poisons the devotee shall duly place a water pot and repeat the Mantra a thousand and eight times. Then he shall pour the water over the victim of poison.

विचरन्विपिनेचौरव्याघ्रसर्पाकुलेनरः ।
जपन्नमुंमंत्रवरंनभयंप्रतिपद्यते ॥१७॥

17. If man has to pass through a forest infested by thieves, tigers and serpents one shall continue to repeat this excellent Mantra. He need not be afraid of any evil consequences.

नौकाः प्रयोगानाह ॥ सहस्रेति । शतपर्वादूवा ॥१४-१७॥

Naukā: 14-17. He explains the rites—Sahasra etc.

Śataparvā = Dūrvā grass.

ईक्षितेनिशिदुःस्वप्नेजपन्मंत्रंनिशांनयेत् ।
अवशिष्टंस्वप्नफलंसस्यगादिशतिध्रुवम् ॥१८॥

18. If any evil dream is seen at night the devotee shall pass the rest of the night repeating the Mantra certainly the bad dream shall become a good dream.

कर्णनेत्रशिरःकंठरोगान्मंत्रोविनाशयेत् ।
अभिचारकृतांपीडांमनुमंत्रितभस्मच ॥१९॥

19. This Mantra destroys all ailments of ears, eyes, head and throat. The ashes inspired by this Mantra remove the affliction due to black magic.

आत्मानंनृहरिंध्यात्वावैरिणंमृगबालकम् ।
आदायप्रक्षिपेद्यस्यांदिशितस्यांसगच्छति ॥२०॥
स्व कुटुंबंपरित्यज्यनचैवावर्त्ततेपुनः ।
नृसिंहं संस्मरन्वादेरिपोःस्वस्यविनष्टये ॥२१॥

प्रजपेदयुतंमंत्रं मारणोत्थाघनष्टये ।
प्रसूनर्बिल्ववृक्षोत्थैः फलैस्तत्काष्ठसंभवैः ॥२२॥
सहस्त्रंजुहुयाद्वह्नौवांछितश्रीसमृद्धये ।
पुत्रजीवेद्धवह्नौतुतत्फलैः पुत्रसंपदे ॥२३॥
ब्राह्मींवचांवामंत्रेणमंत्रितांशतसंख्यया ।
संवत्स रमदन्प्रातर्विद्यापारंगतोभवेत् ॥२४॥
किंबहूक्तेननृहरिः सर्वेष्टफलदोनृणाम् ।

20-24½. The devotee shall conceive himself as Narasimha and a fawn as the enemy. He shall catch hold of that fawn and cast it aside. The enemy will forsake his family and go in the direction the fawn is cast off. He will not return again.

For the destruction of the opponent in the scholarly discusssion the devotee shall (entre the assembly) remembering Narasimha. In order to expiate for the sin of killing (the opponent) the devotee shall repeat the Mantra ten thousand times.

For obtaining the desired prosperity and its further augmentation the devotee shall perform thousand Homas with the flowers, fruits or twigs of Bilva.

For the sake of getting sons the devotee shall perform Homas with the furits of the Putrajīva tree in the fire kindled with the twigs of the same tree.

The devotee shall continuously eat every morning for a year either Brāhmī or Vacā inspired hundred times with the Mantra. He shall become the master of many lores.

Why tell much? Narahari is the bestower of all desired benefits of human beings.

नौकाः निशिदुःस्वप्ने दृष्टे मंत्रंजपन्नवशिष्टांनिशांनयेत् ॥ सदुःस्वप्नः सुस्वप्नस्यैवफलंददाति ॥१८-२१॥

नौका: प्रसंगान्मारणप्रायश्चित्तमाह ।। प्रजपेदिति ।। अभिचारजातपाप-निवृत्त्यैअयुतजपेत् ।।२२।।

Naukā: 18-21. If he has a bad dream at night he shall repeat the Mantra and pass the rest of the night. That bad dream shall bestow the benefit of a good dream.

Naukā: 22. As relevant to the context he explains the expiatory rite for the sin of killing. The devotee shall repeat the Mantra ten thousand times for adoring for the indulgence in black magic and consequent sin.

अथोच्यतेनरहरि र्भीतिहारीष्टसाधकः ।।२५।।
जयद्वयश्रीनृसिंहेत्यष्टार्णोमनुरीरितः ।
ऋषिर्ब्रह्मास्यगायत्रीछंदोदेवो नृकेसरी ।।२६।।
शक्तिर्नेत्रंवियद्बीजमुभेचंद्रसमन्विते ।
वियतादीर्घयुक्तेनचंद्राढ्येनषडंगकम् ।।२७।।

25-27. Now a Mantra of Narahari that removes all fears and accomplishes everything desired is being mentioned. It is of eight syllables as follows :

"Jaya Jaya Śrī Nṛsimha"

The sage of this Mantra is Brahmā and the metre is Gāyatrī. The deity is Nṛkesarī.

Im is the Śakti and Ham is the Bijam.

The Ṣaḍaṅga Nyāsa is to be performed with Hām Hīm Hum Haim Haum and Haḥ.

नौका: पुत्रजीवंवह्वौद्धपुत्रखी वतरुकाष्टैदीप्तेग्नौतत्फलःपुत्रजीवफलैः पुत्राप्त्यैजुहुयात् ।।२३-२५।।

नौका: मंत्रांतरमाहजयेति ।। यथा जय श्रीनृसिंहेति ।।२६।।

नौका: नेत्रंइः शक्तिः ।। वियत्हःबीजम् ।। उभेशक्तिबीजेबिंदुयुते।। दीर्घयुतेनसबिंदुनावियताहेनषंडंगं ।। हांहृत् हींशिरइत्यादि० ।।२७।।

Naukā: 23-25. For the acquisition of sons the devotee shall peform Homas with Putrajīva fruits in the fire kindled with the twigs of the Putrajīva tree.

Naukā: 26. He explains another Mantra *i.e.*

"Jaya Jaya Śrī Nṛsimha" (Be Victorious, O manlion).

Naukā: 27. Netram=I–Śakti

Viyat=Ha–Bijam

Both of them with M added.

The Ṣaḍaṅga has to be perform with Ha in combination with the six long vowels *i.e.*

Hām for Hṛdaya (heart) Hīm for head etc.

श्रीमन्नृकेसरितनोजगदेकबंधोश्रीनीलकंठकरुणार्णवसामराज ।
वह्नींदुतीव्रकरनेत्रपिनाकपाणेशीतांशु शेखररमेश्वरपाहिविष्णो ॥२८॥

28. *Dhyāna Verse.* Protect (everyone) O Viṣṇu, the glorious one, O lord with the form of Man-Lion, the sole kinsman of the univers, the bluenecked one, the ocean of mercy, the lord who manifests himself through the Sāman Mantras, one with the sun, the moon and the fire for eyes, the lord armed with Pināka bow, O lord of Ramā with the moon for adornment of the crest.

नौका: ध्यानमाह ॥ श्रीमदिति ॥ साम्नांराजाईश: ॥ यद्वासामसुराजतेप्रकाशते ससामराज: ॥ सामगानेकृतेप्रत्यक्षोभवतीत्यर्थ: ॥ तीव्रकरो रवि: ॥ पिनाकपाणेइत्युपलक्षणंवराभयचक्राणाम् ॥ वामोर्ध्वादिदक्षोर्ध्वांतपिना- काभयवरचक्रधर इत्यर्थ ॥२८॥

Naukā: 28. *Dhyāna Verse.* Sāmnām (of Sāman mantra) Rājā=Lord or one who shines in the Sāman Verses. That menas the lord becomes perceptible when Sāman Mantra are sung. Tivrakara=Sun. The word Pināka Pāṇi is comprehensive. It includes boon fearlessness and discus as well. Beginning with the left upper hand and ending with the right upper hand the weapons held are Pināka, fearlessness, boon and discus.

एवंध्यात्वाजपेल्लक्षाष्टकंतस्यदशांशतः ।
जुहुयात्पायसेनाग्नौपूजा ह्यस्यतुपूर्ववत् ॥२९॥

29. After meditating thus the devotee shall repeat the Mantra eight hundred thousand times and perform eight thousand Homas in the fire with milk pudding.

नौका: अस्यपूजादिपूजा दिप्रयोगादिकमेकार्णवत् ॥२९॥

Naukā: 29. The worship with this Mantra as well as the special rites etc. same as in the case of the single-syllabled Mantra.

तारः पद्माचहृल्लेखाजयलक्ष्मीपियायच ।
नित्यप्रमुदितांतेतुचेतसेपदमीरयेत् ॥३०॥
लक्ष्मीश्रितार्द्धदेहायरमामायेनमः पदम् ।
एकाधिकस्त्रिंशदर्णोमनुः पद्मभवोमुनिः ॥३१॥
छन्दोतिजगतीप्रोक्तंदेवः श्रीनरकेसरी ।
बीजंरमाद्रिजाशक्तिः श्रीबीजेनषडंगकम् ॥३२॥

30-32. The 31 syllabled Mantra is as follows :

"Om Śrīm Hrīm Jaya Lakṣmīpriyāya Nityapramuditacetasc Lakṣmī Śritārdha Dehyāya Śrī Hrīm Namaḥ"

The sage of this Mantra is the lotus-born deity Brahmā ; the metre is Atijagatī ; and the deity is Śrī Narakesarī.

Śrīm is the Bija and Hrīm is the Śakti. The Ṣaḍaṅga is with Śrīm (with 6 long vowels).

नौका: मंत्रांतरमाह ॥ तार इति ॥ तार ॐ ॥ पद्माश्रीं ॥ हेल्लखाह्रीं ॥३०॥

नौका: रमामाये श्रींह्रीं स्वरूपम न्येत् ॥ यथा-ओंश्रीह्रींजयलक्ष्मीप्रियाय-नित्यप्रसुदितचेतसेलक्ष्मीश्रितार्धदेहायश्रींह्रींनमः ॥ पद्मभवोब्रह्मा ॥३१॥

नौका: अद्रिजाह्रींश्रींबी जेनषड्दार्घयुक्तेनश्रांश्रींश्रूमित्यादिना ॥३२॥

Naukā: 30. He explains another Mantra

Tāra = Om

Padmā = Śrīm

Hṛllekhā=Hrīm.

Naukā: 31. Ramā and Māyā=Śrīm and Hrīm. The rest form itself. Therefore the Mantra is–

"Om Śrīm Hrīm Jaya Lakṣmī Priyāya Nityapramudita Cetase Lakṣmī Śritārdha Dehāya Śrīm Hrīm Namaḥ"

Padma Bhava=Brahmā.

Naukā: 32. Adrijā=Hrīm. Śrīm Bīja with the six long vowels Śrām, Śrīm, Śrūm etc.

क्षीराब्धौवसुमुख्यदेवनिकरैरग्रादिसंवेष्टितः शंखंचक्रगदांबुजंनिज-करैर्बिभ्रंस्त्रिनेत्रः सितः ।

सर्पाधीश फणातपत्रलसितः पीतांबरालंकृतो लक्ष्म्याश्लिष्ट-कलेवरोनरहरिः स्तान्नीलकंठोमुदे ॥३३॥

33. *Dhyāna Verse.* May Lord Narahari be for our joy. He is surrounded in front and other sides with the groups of Devas the chief of whom are the Vasus, in the milk ocean, he holds in the lower arms the conch and the discus, and in the upper arms the club and the lotus, he is white in complexion, he has three eyes, he shines, gloriously with the hood of the Lord of Serpents for his umbrella, he is clad, handsomely in yellow garments, his body is embraced by Lakṣmī and he is blue-throated.

नौका: ध्यानमाह ॥ क्षीराब्धाविति ॥ क्षीरसमुद्रगतश्वेतद्वीपेवश्वादिदेवौघैरग्रादियथावेष्टितः ॥ अग्रेवसुभिः दक्षेरुद्रैः पश्चिमआदित्यैः वामेविश्वदेवैरित्यर्थः ॥ अधोवामदक्षयोः शङ्खचक्रे ॥ ऊर्ध्वयोर्गदापद्मे ॥ सितश्चंद्रवर्ण ॥ शेषफणाएवातपत्रंतेनलसितोदीप्तः ॥ ईदृङ्नृसिंहोम- ममुदेहर्शायस्तात्भूयात् ॥३३॥

Naukā: 33. He explains Dhyāna. In the Śveta island in the milk ocean. He is surrounded by Vasus and other groups of gods in front as well in the directions. In front by the Vasus. In the right by Rudras. In the west by the Ādityas. In the left by Viśvedevas.

In the lower left and right hands the conch and the discus. In the upper–the club and the lotus. Sita=having the colour of the moon. He is brilliantly illuminated by the hood of Śeṣa acting as the Umbrella.

May Nṛsimha of this nature be for my pleasure.

एवंध्या त्वाजपेल्लक्षत्रयषष्टिसहस्त्रकम् ।
मध्वक्तैर्मल्लिकापुष्पैर्जुहुयाज्जातवेदसि ॥३४॥
षट्शतंत्रिसहस्राणिपी ठेपूर्वोदितेयजेत् ।
प्रथमावरणेङ्गानिपरशक्तिरिमाः पुनः ॥३५॥
भास्वतीभास्करीचिंताद्युतिरुन्मीलि नीतथा ।
रमाकांतीरुचिश्चेतिशक्राद्याहेतिसंयुताः ॥३६॥

34-36. After meditating thus the devotee shall repeat the Mantra three hundred and sixty thousand times and perform three thousand and six hundred Homas in the sacred fire with Mallikā flowers soaked in honey. He shall worship in the pedestal mentioned before.

In the first Āvaraṇa the Aṅgas are to be adored. Then (in the second Āvaraṇa) these Śaktis are to be worshipped—They are Bhāsvatī, Bhāskarī, Cintā, Dyuti, Unmīlinī, Ramā, Kānti and Ruci (in the other Āvaraṇa) Indra and others with their respective weapons are to be worshipped.

इत्थंसिद्धेमनौमंत्रीनिग्रहानुग्रहक्षमः ।
मल्लिकाकुसुमैर्होमादिष्टसिद्धिमवाप्नुयात् ॥३७॥

37. When the Mantra has been effectively realized thus, the devotee becomes capable of destroying as well as blessing. He shall attain everything desired by performing Homas with the flowers of Mallikā.

प्रणवोनृहरेर्बीजंनमोभगवतेपदम् ।
नरसिंहायतार क्ष्बीजंमत्स्येतिकीर्तयेत् ॥३८॥

रूपायतारोबीजंचकूर्मरूपायवर्णकाः ।
ताराबीजेवराहार्णारूपायतारबी जके ॥३९॥
नृसिंहरूपायांतेतुतारोबीजंचवामनम् ।
रूपायत्रिस्तारबीजेरामायेतिपदंवदेत् ॥४०॥
तारोबीजंचकृष्णायतारोबीजंचकल्किने ।
जयद्वयंततःशालग्रामदीर्घासनेत्रका ॥४१॥
वासिनेदिव्य सिंहायस्वयंभूङेतिमःस्मृतः ।
पुरुषायनमस्तारोबीजमित्युदितोमनुः ॥४२॥
हरेर्नवनवत्यर्णोमुनि रत्रिः किलास्यतु ।
छंदोतिजगतीदेवोनृकेसर्य्यवतारवान् ॥४३॥
बीजंपूर्वोदितंशक्तिराद्याबीजेन चांगकम् ।
कृत्वाषड्दीर्घयुक्तेनध्यायेत्क्षीरोदधिस्थितम् ॥४४॥

38-44. The next Mantra is of ninety-nine syllables as follows :

"Om Kṣraum Namo Bhagavate Narasimhāya, Om Kṣraum Matsyarūpāya, Om Kṣraum Kūrmarūpāya, Om Kṣraum Varāharūpāya, Om Kṣraum Nṛsimharūpāya, Om Kṣraum Vāmanarūpāya, Om Kṣraum Om Kṣraum Om Kṣraum Rāmāya, Om Kṣraum Kṛṣṇāya, Om Kṣraum Kalkine Jaya Jaya Śālāgrāmanivāsine Divyasimhāya Svayambhuve Puruṣāya Namaḥ Om Kṣraum" [Daśavatāra Nṛsiṁhā Mantra].

The sage of this ninety-nine syllabled Mantra is Atri, the metre is Atijagatī; the deity is the incarnation of the Man-Lion. The Bīja is mentioned before (*i.e.* Kṣraum) and Om is the Śakti. The Ṣaḍaṅga Nyāsa is to be performed with the Bīja with the six long vowels. Thereafter he shall meditate on the Lord stationed in the Milk-ocean.

नौकाः मंत्रांतरमाह ॥ प्रणवइति ॥ नृहरेर्बीजक्ष्रौं ॥३८-३९॥

नौका: त्रिस्त्रिवारंताबीजे ।।४०।।

नौका: सनेत्रादीर्घाइयुतोनः नि ।।४१।।

नौका: ङेतिमश्चतुर्थ्यंतः ।।४२।।

नौका: नवनवत्यर्णएकोनशताक्षरः ।। मंत्रोयथा-ओक्षंरौंनमोभगवतेनरसिंहाय ओंक्ष्रौंमत्स्यरूपायओंक्ष्रौंकूर्मरूपायओंक्ष्रौंवराहरूपायओंक्ष्रोंनृसिंहरूपायओंक्ष्रौंवामन-रूपायओंक्ष्रौंओंक्ष्रौंओंक्ष्रौंरामायओंक्ष्रौं कृष्णायओंक्ष्रौंकल्किनेजयजयशालग्रामनिवासिने-दिव्यसिंहायस्वयंभुवेपुरुषायनमः ओंक्ष्रौं ।। अवतारवान्दशावतारयुतोनृसिंहोदेवता ।।४३।।

Naukā: 38-39. He explains another Mantra. The Bīja of Nṛhari is Kṣraum.

Naukā: 40. Triḥ=Three times—The Praṇava and the Bīja.

Naukā: 41. Sanetra Dīrghā=Na+I=Ni.

Naukā: 42. Ṅntima=ending in the dative case.

Naukā: 43. Navanavatyarṇa=Having 90 syllables. The Mantra is as follows :

"Om Kṣraum Namo Bhagavate Narasimhāya Om Kṣraum Matsyasvarūpāya Om Kṣraum Kūrmarūpāya, Om Kṣraum Varāharūpāya Om Kṣraum Nṛsimharūpāya Om Kṣraum Vāmanarūpāya Om Kṣraum Om Kṣraum Om Kṣraum Rūpāya Om Kṣraum Kṛṣṇāya Om Kṣraum Kalkine Jaya Jaya Śālagrāma Nivāsine Divyasimhāya Svayambhuve Puruṣāya Namaḥ Om Kṣraum"

Avatāravān=The deity is Nṛsimha of ten incarnations

सहस्त्रचंद्रप्रतिमोदयालुर्लक्ष्मीमु खालोकनलोलनेत्रः ।
दशावतारैःपरितः परीतोनृकेसरीमंगलमातनोतु ।।४५।।

45. *Dhyāna Verse.* May the compassionate Nṛkesarī bestow auspiciousness. He resembles a thousand moons (in brilliance); his eyes are earger to look at Lakṣmī and he is surrounded on all sides by the ten incarnations.

जपोयुतंदशांशेनह वनंपायसेनतु ।
पीठेपूर्वोदितेपूर्वमंगानिपरिपूजयेत् ।।४६।।

दशावतारान्मत्स्यादीन्दिक्पालानायु धान्यपि ।
प्रयोगाः पूर्ववत्प्रोक्ताः सर्वसिद्धिप्रदेमनौ ॥४७॥

46-47. The Mantra is to be repeated ten thousand times and a thousand Homas are to be performed with milk pudding. As before the Aṅgas are to be worshipped in the pedestal. Thereafter the ten incarnations beginning with the fish, the guardians of the quarters and their weapons are to be worshiped. The special rites are as mentioned before when the Mantra has been adequately practised to be capable of according supernatural powers.

नौकाः ओंक्ष्रौंबीजम् ॥ आद्येति ॥ ओंशक्तिः ॥ क्ष्रांक्ष्रीमित्याद्यंगम् ॥४४-४७॥

Naukā: 44-47. Om Ksraum is the Bīja. Ādyā=Om Om is the Sakti.

The Aṅga Nyāsa is with Kṣrām, Kṣrīm etc.

अथाभयनृसिंहमंत्रः ।
तारोनमोभगवतेनरसिंहायहृच्च्वते ।
जस्तेजसेआविराविर्भववज्रनखांततः ॥४८॥
वज्रदंष्ट्रचक्रर्मातित्वाशयान्रंधयद्वयम् ।
तमोग्रसद्वयंवह्नेःकलत्रमभयंपुनः ॥४९॥
आत्मन्यंतेचभूयिष्ठास्तारोबीजंमनुःस्मृतः ।
द्विषष्ट्यर्णैःशुकः प्रोक्तोमुनिश्छंदस्तुपूर्ववत् ॥५०॥
अभयो नारसिंहस्तुदेवतान्यत्तुपूर्ववत् ।
अथगोपालमनवः प्रोच्यंतेस्वेष्टसाधकाः ॥५१॥

48-51. *Abhaya Nṛsiṁha Mantra.* This mantra is of sixtytwo syllables as follows :

"Om Namo Bhagavate Narasimāya Namastejastejase Āvirāvirbhava Vajra Nakha Vajra Daṁṣṭra Karmāśayān Randhaya Randhaya Tamo Grasa Grasa Svāhā Abhayamātmani Bhūyiṣṭhā Om Kṣraum"

The sage of this Mantra is Śuka. The metre is as

before. The deity is Abhaya Nārasiṁha. The other factors are as before.

Now Gopāla Mantras are being explained. They enable us to realize our cherished desires.

नौका: मत्रांतरमाह ।। तारइति ।। हृन्नम: ।।४८।।

नौका: वह्नेः कलत्रं स्वाहा ।।४९।।

नौका: बीजंक्ष्रौं ।। यथा-ओंनमोभगवतेनरसिंहायनमस्तेजस्तेजसे आविराविर्भववज्रनस्ववज्रदंष्ट्रकर्माशयान्त्रन्धय २ तमोग्रस २ स्वाहाअभयमात्मनिभूयिष्ठाओंक्ष्रौंमिति ।।५०।।

नौका: अन्यत्पूजादि ।।५१।।

Naukā: 48. He explains another Mantra Hṛt=Namaḥ.

Naukā: 49. Vahneḥ Kalatram – Svāhā.

Naukā: 50. Bījam=Kṣraum. The Mantra is :

"Om Namo Bhagavate Narasimhāya Namastejastejase Āvirāvirbhava Vajra Nakha Vajra Daṁṣṭra Karmāśayān Randhaya Randhaya Tamo Grasa Grasa Svāhā Abhayamātmani Bhūyiṣṭha Om Kṣraum"

Naukā: 51. Anyat – other things – Pūjām etc.

गोपीजनपद स्यांतेवल्लभायाग्निसुंदरी ।

दशाक्षरोमनुःप्रोक्तोमनोरथफलप्रदः ।।५२।।

52. The ten syllabled Gopāla Mantra is as follows : "Gopījana Vallabhāya Svāha"

It bestows the benefits desired.

नौका: गोपालमंत्रमाह ।। गोपीति ।। अग्निसुंदरीस्वाहा ।। यथा-गोपीजनवल्लभायस्वाहा ।।५२।।

Naukā: 52. He explains Gopāla mantra. Agni Sundarī=Svāhā. The mantra is –

"Gopījana Vallabhāya Svāhā".

नारदोस्यविराट्कृष्णोमु निपूर्वाः समीरिताः ।
बीजशक्तीतुविज्ञेयेक्रमात्कामानलप्रिये ॥५३॥

53. The sage of this Mantra is Nārada. The metre is Virāṭ and Kṛṣṇa in the deity, Klīm is the Bīja and Svāhā is the Śakti.

नौका: विराट्छंदः ॥ क्लींबींज ॥ स्वाहा शक्तिः ॥५३॥

Naukā: 53. The metre is Virāṭ. Klīm is the Bīja. Svāhā is Śakti.

आचक्रायहृदाख्यातंविचक्रायशिरोपिच ।
सुचक्रायशिखापश्चात्रैलोक्यरक्षणंततः ॥५४॥
चक्राय कवचंप्रोक्तमसुरांतकशब्दतः ।
चक्रायास्त्रमिदंकुर्य्यादंगानांपंचकंमनोः ॥५५॥

54-55. This has only Pañāṅga Nyāsa as follows :

Obeisance unto the heart, unto Ācakra

Svāhā unto the head, unto Vicakra

Vaṣaṭ unto the tuft, unto Sucakra

Hum unto the armour, unto Trailokya Rakṣaṇacakra

Phaṭ unto the Astra, unto Asurāntakacakra.

नौका: पचांगमाह ॥ आचक्रायहृत् ॥ विचक्रायशिरः ॥ ॥ सुचक्रायशिखा ॥ त्रैलोक्यरक्षणचक्रायकवचम् ॥ आसुरांतकचक्रायअस्त्रम् ॥५४॥

Naukā: 54-54. Ācakrāya – heart

Vicakrāya – head

Trailokya Rakṣaṇacakrāya – armour

Sucarkrāya – tuft

Asurāntakacakrāya – Astra.

सर्वांगेत्रिमनुंन्यस्य वर्णन्यासंसमाचरेत् ।
मस्तकेनेत्रयोःश्रुत्योनसोर्वक्रेहृदंबुजे ॥५६॥

जठरेलिंगदेशेचजानुनो:पाद योरपि ।
वर्णांस्तारपुटान्न्यस्येद्विंद्वाड्यान्नमसायुतान् ॥५७॥

56-57. At the outset the devotee utters the Mūla Mantra three times and performs Nyāsa all over the body. Then he must perform Varṇa Nyāsa. Each syllable of the Mantra is uttered with Anusvāra and Om at the beginning and after (As a Sampuṭa). The places for Nyāsa are head, eyes, ears, nose, mouth, heart, belly, penis, knees and feet and the word Namaḥ is added with all of them e.g.

Om Gom Namaḥ—on the head

Om Pim Namaḥ—on the eyes

Om Jam Namaḥ—on the ears etc. etc.

नौका: वर्णन्यासमाह ॥ मस्तकइति ॥५६॥

नौका: तारपुटानिति ॥ ओंगों ओंनम:मस्तके ओं पींओनम:नेत्रयोरित्यादि० ॥५७॥

Naukā: 56. He explains Varṇa Nyāsa.

Naukā: 57. With Tāra for Sampuṭa. Hence

Om Gom Om obeisance—on the head

Om Pīm Om obeisance—in the eyes.

वृंदारण्यगकल्पपादपतलेसद्रत्नपीठेंबु जेशोणाभेवसुपत्रकेस्थित-मजंपीतांबरालंकृतम् ।
जीमूताभमनेकभूषणयुतंगोगोपगोपीवृतंगोविंदंस्मरसुंद रंमुनियुतं-वेणुंरणंतंस्मरेत् ॥५८॥

58. *Dhyāna Verse.* One should remember the unborn immortal Govinda playing on the flute. He is stationed on an eight petalled red lotus above a gem set pedestal beneath the Kalpa tree in the sylvan surroundings of Vṛndāvana. He is clad in yellow garments. He has the lustre of the cloud. He has a number of ornaments. He is surrounded by cow

cowherds and cowherdesses and accompanied by sages. He is as handsome as the god of love.

नौकाः ध्यानमाह ।। वृन्दावनगतकल्पवृक्षतलेमणिपीठेरक्ताष्टपत्रेस्थितंध्यायेत् ।। जीमूताभंमेघश्यामंस्मरादपिसुंदरम् ।।५८।।

Naukā: 58. *Dhyāna Verse.* He explains Dhyāna. The devotee should meditate on the lord seated on the red eight petalled lotus on the same gem set pedestal beneath the Kalpavṛksa in the forest of Vṛndāvana Jimūtābham = Resembling cloud – dark complexioned. He is more handsome than even god of Love.

एवंध्यात्वाजपेल्लक्षंदशांशंसरसीरुहैः ।
जुहुयात्पूजयेत्पीठंवैष्णवे नंदनंदनम् ।।५९।।

59. After meditating thus he shall repeat the Mantra a hundred thousand times and perform ten thousand Homas with lotuses. He shall worship Nanda's child on the Vaiṣṇava pedestal.

अग्न्यादिकोणेष्वश्यर्च्यहृदाद्यंगचतुष्टयम् ।
दिशास्वस्त्रंदलेष्वष्टौमहिषीः परिपूज येत् ।।६०।।
रुक्मिणीसत्यभामाचनग्नजित्तनयार्कजा ।
मित्रविंदालक्ष्मणाचजांबवत्यासुशीलका ।।६१।।
महि ष्योष्टौसुवर्णाभाविचित्राभरणस्त्रजः ।
दलाग्रेवसुदेवंचदेवकींनंदगोपितम् ।।६२।।
यशोदाबलभद्रंच सुभद्रांगोपगोपिकाः ।
इंद्रादीनपिवज्रादीन्पूजयेत्तदनंतरम् ।।६३।।

60-63. The four Aṅgas beginning with the heart should be worshipped in the corners south-east etc. and the Astra in the quarters. The devotee then worships the crowned queens (of Kṛṣṇa) in the petals. They are Rukmiṇī, Satyabhāmā, the daughter of Nagnajit, Kālindī, Mitravindā, Lakṣmaṇā, Jāmbavatī and Suśīlā. The eight queen should be conceived as gold complexioned and having diverse kinds of ornaments and garlands.

At the tips of the petals Vasudeva, Devakī, Nandagopa, Yaśodā, Balabhadra, Subhadrā, the cowherds and the cowherdesses should be worshipped.

Thereafter Indra and the other guardians of the quarters and the thunderbolt and other weapons should be worshipped.

नौका: अर्कजाकालिंदी ।।६१-६२।।

Naukā: 61-62. Arkajā=Kālindī.

इत्थंसिद्धेमनौमंत्रीसाधयेत्स्वमनी षितम् ।
गुडूचीशकलैरग्नौजुहुयाज्ज्वरशांतये ।।६४।।

64. When the Mantra has been perfectly realized thus the devotee can go ahead with the rites for the realization of his desires.

In order to quell fevers the devotee shall perfrom pieces of Guḍūcī in the fire.

कृष्णंद्वेषंप्रकुर्वंतंबलदेवस्यरुक्मिण: ।
द्यूता सक्तस्यसंचिंत्यगोमयोद्भवगोलकान् ।।६५।।
जुहुयाद्द्वेषसिद्ध्यर्थंनरयो:सुहृदोर्मिथ: ।
पिचुमंदफ लोत्पन्नतैलाश्यक्तै:समिद्वरै: ।।६६।।
अक्षजैर्जुहुयाद्रात्रावयुतंशत्रुशांतये ।
अयुतंप्रजपेन्मंत्रमात्मानं संस्मरन्हरिम् ।।६७।।
मंचस्त्रस्तगतप्राणाकृष्टकंसंरिपुंसुधी: ।
शत्रुजन्मर्क्षवृक्षोत्थसमिद्भिरयुतंनिशि ।।६८।।
जुहुयादित्थमुग्रोपिसपत्नोनिधनंव्रजेत् ।
पलाशकुसुमैर्लक्षंविद्यासिद्ध्यैजुहोतुना ।।६९।।

65-69. In order to accomplish the estrangement between two friends, the devotee shall meditate on Kṛṣṇa as being angry with Balabhadra and Rukmiṇī engrossed in playing the game of dice and perform the Homas with balls of dried cowdung.

For the quelling of enemies the devotee shall at night perform ten thousand Homas with the twigs of Akṣa trees smeared with margosa oil.

The intelligent devotee shall repeat the Mantra ten thousand times meditating on Hari, identifying himself with the lord and the enemy with Kāmsa who had been dragged (by the lord) and who slipped down from his conch with vital airs extinct and perform ten thousand Homas at night with the twigs from the tree corresponding to the star of the enemy [IX-50]. If this is properly done even the fierce enemy shall die.

For the purpose of achieving learning, the man shall perform a hundred thousand Homas with the Palāśa flowers.

नौका: गोपाश्चगोपिकाश्चता: ।।६३-६७।।

Naukā: 63-67. The cowherds as well as cowherdesses.

तंडुलैः सितपुष्पाद्यैराज्याक्तैःप्रत्यहंनरः ।
हुत्वासप्तदिनांतेतद्भस्मभालेचमूर्द्धनि ।।७०।।
धारयन्वशयेत्सद्योयौवतंतच्चपूरुषान् ।।
पुष्पंवासोंजनंवापितांबूलमथचंदनम् ।।७१।।
सहस्त्रंमनुना जप्तंदद्याद्यस्मैनरायसः ।
वशमेत्यचिरादेवसपुत्रपशुबांधवः ।।७२।।

70-72. The intelligent devotee shall regularly perform Homas with rice grains mixed with mustard and also with white flowers etc. At the end of seven days he shall apply the ashes thereof on his forehead and head. This enables him to exercise a fascinating control over groups of young women instantneously young women doing like this shall control men.

If flowers, garments collyrium, betel leaf, sandal paste etc. inspired thousand times with this Mantra is given to anyone he shall erelong come under the influence of the devotee along with his sons, kinsmen and cattle-wealth.

नौकाः मंचात् स्रस्तोगतप्राणआकुष्ठश्चासौकंस श्चतथाभूतंरिपुस्मरन् ।। रिपुजन्मनक्षत्रवृक्षसमिद्भिर्जुहुयात् ।। नक्षत्रवृक्षाउक्ताः ।।६८-७०।।

Naukā: 68-70. Kaṁsa had slipped down from the conch and his life was extinct. He was dragged also The enemy should be meditated upon thus. He shall perform Homas with the twigs of the tree corresponding to the Birth Star of the enemy. Thos trees have been enumerated [IX-50].

वृंदावनस्थंगायंतंगोपीभिः सं स्मरन्हरिम् ।
अपामार्गसमिद्भिर्योजुहुयाद्वशयेज्जगत् ।।७३।।

73. He who meditates on Hari stationed in Vṛndavana and engaged in singing along with the cowherd lasses and performs Homas with the twigs of Apāmārga shall fascinate the entire universe.

रासक्रीडागतंकृष्णंध्यायन्योयुतमा जपेत् ।
षण्मसाद्वांछितांकन्यामुद्वहेद्भक्तितत्परः ।।७४।।

74. The devout man shall meditate on Kṛṣṇa engaged in Rāsakrīḍā and repeat the Mantra ten thousand times. He shall marry the girl of his choice within six months.

नौकाः तच्चयौवतं युवतिसमूहः पुरुषान्वशयेत् ।।७१-७४।।

Naukā: 71-74. That group of young women can enchant men.

जपेत्सहस्त्रंध्यायंतीयाकदंबस्थितंहरिम् ।
कन्यकावांछितंनाथंमण्डलांतर्लभेतसा ।।७५।।

75. The girl who meditate on Hari seated on the Kadamba tree and repeats the Mantra thousand times

(everyday) shall obtain the desired husband within a Maṇḍala (49 days).

पत्रैःफलैःसमिद्भिर्वाबिल्वोत्त्थैर्मधुसंयुतैः ।
कमलैःशर्क रायुक्तैर्होमाल्लक्ष्मीपतिर्भवेत् ॥७६॥
बहुनाकिमिहोक्तेनकृष्णः सर्वार्थदोनृणाम् ।
अथमंत्रांतरंघच्मिगो विंदस्येष्टदंनृणाम् ॥७७॥

76-77. By performing Homas with the leaves, fruits or twigs of the Bilva tree mixed with honey or with lotuses mixed with sugar the devotee shall be the lord of wealth.

Why tell much? Kṛṣṇa is the bestower of all objects to men.

I shall now explain another Mantra of Govinda that bestows desired things to men.

नौका: मंडलमेकोनपंचाशद्दिनानितन्मध्येवांछितंप्रियंप्राप्नोति ॥७५॥

Naukā: 75-77. Maṇḍala=49 days. In the course of those days she will get the desired lover.

कामोवियद्रेचिकाढ्यः पीतावामाक्षिसंयुताः ।
चक्रीझिंटीशमारूढोबकोनंतान्वि तोमरुत् ॥७८॥
हृदयांतोमनुश्रेष्ठोवसुवर्णोखिलेष्टदः ।
मुनिःसम्मोहनाद्योस्यनारदः परिकीर्तितः ॥७९॥
गायत्रीछंदइत्युक्तंदेवस्त्रैलोक्यमोहनः ।
कामबीजेनषड्दीर्घयुक्तेनांगंसमाचरेत् ॥८०॥

78-80. The eight syllabled Mantra of Govinda is as follows :

"Klīm Hṛṣī Keśāya Namaḥ"

It bestows everything desired.

The sage of this Mantra is Sammohananārada, the metre is Gāyatrī and the deity is Trailokyamohana.

The Ṣadaṅga Nyāsa is to be performed with the Klīm.Bīja in combination with the six vowels (long).

नौका: मंत्रांतरमाह ।। कामइति ।। काम:क्लीं ।। वियत्‌ह:रेचिकाढ्य: ऋयुत: हृ ।। पीताष: वामाक्षिसंयुताईयुता षी ।। चक्रीक झिंटीशए तदारूढ:के ।। वक:श: अनंतान्वित: आयुता:शा: ।। मरुत्‌य: ।।७८।।

नौका: हृदयंनम: ।। यथा-क्लींहृषीकेशायनम: ।।७९।।

नौका: षडंगमाह ।। कामेति ।। क्लांहृत्‌ क्लींशिरइत्यादि० ।।८०।।

Naukā: 78. He explains another Mantra–

Kāma=Klīm

Viyat=ha

Recikāḍhy=Having Ṛ. Hence Hṛ

Pītā=Ṣa

Vāmākṣi Samyutā=Having Ī *i.e.* Ṣī

Cakrī=Ka

Jhiṇṭīsa=E mounting it. Hence Ke

Baka=Śa

Anantānvita–Having Ā. Hence Śā

Marut=Ya

Naukā: 79. Hṛdayam=Namaḥ The Mantra is

"Klīm Hṛṣīkeśāya Namaḥ"

Naukā: 80. He explains Ṣaḍaṅga–

Klām for heart. Klīm for head etc.

कल्पानो कहमूलसंस्थितवयोराजोन्नतांसंस्थितंपौष्पंबाणमथेक्षुचाप-कमलेपाशांकुशेबिभ्रतम् ।

चक्रंशंखगदेकरै रुदधिजासंश्लिष्टदेहहरिं नानाभूषणरक्तलेपकुसुमं-पीतांबरंसंस्मरेत् ।।८१।।

81. *Dhyāna Verse.* One shall meditate on Hari clad in yellow garments. He is seated on the lofty shoulders of the

king of birds (Garuḍa) perched on the roots of the Kalpa tree; he holds in his four right hands the floral arrow, lotus, goad and the conch and in the left hands the sugarcane bow, noose, discus and the club; his body is hold in embrace by the daughter of the ocean (*i.e.* Lakṣmī) and he is adorned with flowers, different kinds of ornaments and red sandal paste.

नौकाः ध्यानमाह ।। कल्पेति ।। कल्पवृक्षमूलस्थितगरुडासनबाणपद्मांकुशशंखा दक्षेषु । अन्यान्यन्येषु ।।८१।।

Naukā: 81. *Dhyāna Verse.* He explains Dhyāna. He is seated on Garuḍa stationed beneath the Kalpa tree. In the right hands—Arrow, lotus, goad and conch. The other weapons to the other hands.

एवंध्यात्वाजपेत्यसूर्यलक्षं त्रिमधुरप्लुतैः ।
पलाशपुष्पैर्जुहुयात्तत्सहस्त्रंहुताशने ।।८२।।
तर्पयेत्सलिलैस्तावत्पीठेपूर्वोदितेयजेत् ।
पक्षिराजायठद्वंद्वमनेनगरुडार्चनम् ।।८३।।

82-83. After meditating thus the devotee shall repeat the Mantra one million and two hundred thousand times and perform twelve thousand times the Homas with Palāśa flowers soaked in three sweets (honey, ghee, sugar). Thereafter he shall offer libations as many times (twelve thousand times). Then he shall worship in the pedestal mentioned before. The worship of Garuḍa is with the Mantra "Pakṣirājāya Svāhā".

नौकाः सूर्यलंक्षद्वादशलक्षम् ।।८२।।

Naukā: 82. Sūryalakṣa=One million two hundred thousand.

मुकुटंशिरसीष्ट्वाथकर्णयोःकुंडलेयजेत् ।
करेषुचक्रं द्यस्त्राणिश्रीवत्संकौस्तुभंहृदि ।।८४।।

वनमालांगलेश्रोणीदेशेपीतांबरंश्रियम् ।
वामांगेश्यर्च्यवह्नया दिदिग्विदिक्ष्वंगपूजनम् ॥८५॥
दिक्षुप्रपूज्यचतुरोबाणान्कोणेषुपंचमम् ।
लक्ष्म्याद्याः शक्तयःपूज्याः शक्राद्याआयुधान्यपि ॥८६॥
लक्ष्मीः सरस्वतीचापिरतिः प्रीतिश्चतुर्थिका ।
कीर्तिः कांतिस्तु ष्टिपुष्टीइतिलक्ष्म्यादयोमताः ॥८७॥

84-87. Thereafter he shall begin these worships of the ancillaries as follows :

The crown is to be worshipped in the head, the earrings in the ears, the weapons discus etc. in the hands, Śrīvatsa and Kaustubha in the heart, the garland of Sylvan flowers in the neck, the yellow garment in the hips and Śrī in the left side.

Thereafter the Aṅgas are to be worshipped in the interquarters such as south-east etc. and in all the quarters (collectively).

The four arrows are worshipped in the quarters and the fifth one in all the corners.

Afterwards the Śaktis beginning with Lakṣmī are to be worshipped. They are : Lakṣmī, Sarasvatī, Rati, Prīti, Kīrti, Kānti, Tuṣti and Puṣṭi.

Afterwards Indra and others as well as thunderbolt and other weapons are to be worshipped.

विजयापुष्पसंयुक्तैर्जलैःसंतर्पयेच्छतम् ।
प्रातःप्रत्यहमेतस्यवांछितंमासतोभवेत् ॥८८॥
अयुतंतुघृतेना ग्नौहुत्वासंपातजंघृतम् ।
तावज्जप्तंप्रियाकांतंभोजयेदृशमेतिसः ॥८९॥

88-89. The devotee shall offer hundred libations everyday in the morning with waters along with Vijayā flowers. Within a mouth he will realize his desired objects.

The devotee shall perform ten thousand Homas with ghee and the residue ghee should be inspired ten thousand times with the Mantra. If a woman offers this ghee to her husband for drinking he will come under her control.

ठद्वयंस्वाहा ॥८३-८९॥

Naukā: 83-89. Ṭhadvayam=Svāhā.

कामबीजेपिविज्ञेयापरिच र्य्योक्तमंत्रवत् ।
विशेषात्कामिनीवर्गमोहकोमनुनायकः ॥९०॥

90. "Klīm" is a single syllabled Mantra. The mode of worship with this Mantra is the same as mentioned before. It is a leader among mantras and especially efficacious in the case of enchanting lovely women.

नौका: मंत्रांतरमाह ॥ कामेति ॥ क्लीमिति गोपालमनुः परिचर्येति ॥ तत्पूजोक्ताष्टार्णवदित्यर्थः ॥ अयंस्त्रीवशीकारी ॥९०॥

Naukā: 90. He explains another Mantra. Klīm is Gopāla Mantra. Paricaryā – Worship is like that of the eight syllabled one. This Mantra is capable of attracting women.

रमाभवानीकंदर्पःकृष्णायस्मृतिरो युता।
विंदायवह्निजायांतोद्वादशार्णोमनुःस्मृतः ॥९१॥

91. The twelve syllabled Mantra is as follows :
"Śrīm Hrīm Kṛṣṅāya Govindāya Svāhā".

नौका: मंत्रांतरमाह ॥ रमेति ॥ रमाश्रीं ॥ भवानीह्रीं ॥ कंदर्पःक्लीं स्मृतिर्गः ओयुता गो ॥ यथा-श्रींह्रींक्लींकृष्णायगोविंदाय स्वाहेति ॥९१॥

Naukā: 91. He explains another Mantra

Ramā=Śrīm

Bhavanī=Hrīm

Kandarpa=Klīm

Smṛti=Ga

Oyutā – having O Hence Go

The Mantra is –

"Śrīm Hrīm Klīm Kṛṣṇāya Govindāya Svāha".

मुनिर्ब्रह्मास्यगायत्रीछंदःकृष्णोस्यदेवता ।

धरैकचंद्र रामाब्धिनेत्रार्णैरंगमीरितम् ॥९२॥

उपासनास्यमंत्रस्यपूर्ववत्परिकीर्त्तिता ।

अथवक्ष्येषोडशार्णमनुंलोकवि मोहनम् ॥९३॥

92-93. The sage of this Mantra is Brahmā the metre is Gāyatrī and the deity is Kṛṣṇa. The Ṣaḍaṅga Nyāsa is to be performed with the syllables of the Mantra split at 1, 1, 1, 3, 4 and 2. The mode of worship of this Mantra is as mentioned before.

Now I shall mention another Mantra of sixteen syllables, that facinates all the words.

नौका: षडंगमाह ॥ धरैकेति ॥ धराएकः ॥९२-९३॥

Naukā: 92-93. He explains Ṣaḍaṅga Nyāsa. Dharā - one.

अथरुक्मिणीवल्लभमंत्रः ।

तारोहृद्भगवतेंतेरुक्मिणीङेन्तवल्लभः ।

द्विठांतःषोडशार्णोयंनारदो मुनिरस्यतु ॥९४॥

छन्दोनुष्टुब्देवतातुरुक्मिणीवल्लभोहरिः ।

एकद्वियुगसप्ताक्षिवणःपचांगमीरितम् ॥९५॥

94-95. It is as follows :

"Om Namo Bhagavate Rukmiṇīvallabhāya Svāhā"

The sage of this Mantra is Nārada, the metre is Anuṣṭup and the deity is Hari the lover of Rukmiṇī. The five Aṅga Nyāsas are to be performed with the syllables of the Mantra split at 1, 2, 4, 7 and 2.

नौकाः मंत्रांतरमाह ।। तारइति ।। ॐनमोभगवतेरुक्मिणी वल्लभायस्वाहेति ।।९४।।

नौकाः पंचागमाह ।। एकेति ।।९५।।

Naukā: 94. He explains another Mantra e.g.

"Om Namo Bhagavate Rukmiṇī Vallabhāya Svāhā"

Naukā: 95. Pañcāṅga is explained.

चिंताश्मयुक्तनिजदोः परिरब्धकांतमालिंगितंसजलजेनकरेणपत्न्या ।
सौवर्णवेत्रयुतहस्तमनेकभूषंपीतां बरंभजतकृष्णमभीष्टसिद्ध्यै ।।९६।।

96. *Dhyāna Verse.* Oye all, resort to Kṛṣṇa for the achievement of everything desired. He has held his wife in embrace with his hand holding the Cintāmaṇi stone. He is embraced by his wife with her hand holding the lotus. In the (other) hand he holds a golden stick. He is clad in yellow garments and wears many ornaments.

नौकाः ध्यानमाह ।। चिंतेति ।। चिंतामणियुतनिजहस्तेनालिंगिताकांतायेनतम् ।। सपद्महस्तयापत्न्यालिंगितं ।। स्वर्णयष्टियुतद्क्षकरम् ।।९६।।

Naukā: 96. *Dhyāna Verse.* He explains Dhyāna. The beloved is held in embrace by him with his hand holding the gem Cintāmaṇi. He himself is hold in embrace by his wife holding the lotus in her hand. The right hand holds golden beton.

लक्षंजपेद्दशांशेनपद्मैर्होमंसमाचरेत् ।
अंगैर्नारदवृत्रारिवज्राद्यैः पूजयेद्धरिम् ।।९७।।
नारदंपर्वतंजिष्णुनिशठोद्धवदारुकान् ।
विष्वक्सेनंचशैनेयंदिक्ष्वग्रेविनतासु तम् ।।९८।।

97-98. The devotee shall repeat the Mantra a hundred thousand times and perform ten thousand Homas with lotuses. Hari is to be worshipped along with the worship of the Aṅgas, Nārada, Indra, the thunderbolt etc.

The following are to be worshipped in the quarters

and Garuḍa in front. They are Nārada, Parvata, Jiṣṇu, Niśaṭha, Uddhava, Dāruka, Viṣvaksena and Śaineya.

नौका: अंगैर्नारदादिभि: ।। इन्द्रादिभि: वज्रादिभि: ।।९७-९८।।

Naukā: 97-98. Aṅgaiḥ—*i.e.*Nārada and others, Indra and others, thunderbolt etc.

अथाष्टाक्षरी ।

कामोगोवल्लभोङेन्त:स्वाहांतोष्टाक्षरोमनु: ।

गायत्रीकृष्णधातारश्छंदो देवर्षयोमता: ।

वर्णयुग्मै:समस्तेनपंचांगविधिरीरित: ।।९९।।

99-103. The eight syllabled Mantra is as follows :

"Klīm Govallabhāya Svāhā"

The sage is Dhātā, the metre is Gāyatrī and the deity is Kṛṣṇa The Pañcāṅga Nyāsa is to be performed with pairs of syllables (the first four cases) and collectively in the case of Astra.

नौका: मंत्रातंरमाह ।। कामइति ।। क्लींगोवल्लभायस्याहेति ।। गायत्रीछन्द: ।। कृष्णोदेवता ।। ब्रह्मात्र्रषि: ।। पंचांगमाह ।। वर्णेति ।। क्लींगोहृत् ।। वल्लशिर: ।। भायशिखा ।। स्वाहावर्म ।। सर्वेणास्त्रम ।।९९।।

Naukā: 99. He explains another Mantra *i.e.*

"Klīm Go Vallabhāya Svāhā".

The metre is Gāyatrī. The deity is Kṛṣṇa. The sage is Brahmā. Pañcāṅga is explained

Klīm Go - heart

Valla - head

Bhāya - tuft

Svāhā - armour

With the entire Mantra - Astra.

हरिंपंचवर्षव्रजेधावमानंस्वसौंदर्यसं मोचितंस्वर्गयोषम् ।

यशोदासुतंस्त्रीगणैर्दृष्टकेलिंभजेभूषितंभूषणैनुपुराद्यै: ।।१००।।

100. *Dhyāna Verse.* I worship Hari the five year old son of Yaśoda who is running about in the cowherds' colony of Vraja who has fascinated the celastial damsels by means of his handsome features, whose playful pranks are eagerly witnessed by the groups of women and who is bedecked in anklets and other ornaments.

The devotee shall repeat the Mantra eight hundred times and perform eight thousand Homas with the excellent twigs of Brahma Vṛksa (Palāś). he Aṅgas are to be worshipped as before. Then in the quarters and interval spaces the following are to be worshipped viz. – Vāsudeva, Saṁkarṣaṇa, Pradyumna, Aniruddha, Rukmiṇī, Satyabhāmā, Lakṣmaṇā and Jāmbavatī.

Thereafter Indra and others are to be worshipped as well as thunderbolt and other weapons.

When the Mantra has thus been perfectly realized the devotee shall become the abode of riches.

अष्टलक्षंजपेदष्टसहस्त्रं ब्रह्मवृक्षजैः ।
समिद्वरैः प्रजुहुयादंगार्चादिग्विदिक्ष्वथ ॥१०१॥
वासुदेवःसंकर्षणः प्रद्युम्नश्चानिरुद्धकः ।
रुक्मिणीसत्यभामाचलक्ष्मणाजांबवत्यपि ॥१०२॥
संक्रंद नादयःपूज्यावज्राद्यान्यायुधानिच ।
एवंसिद्धेमनौमंत्रीसंपदामालयोभवेत् ॥१०३॥
कामसंपुटितंकृष्ण पदंवेदाक्षरोमनुः ।
गायत्रीनारदःकृष्णश्छंदोमुनिरधीश्वरः ॥१०४॥
दीर्घारूढेनकामेनषडंगन्यासमा चरेत् ।
कल्पद्रुमूलसंरूढपद्मस्थंचिंतयेद्धरिम् ॥१०५॥

104-105. The four syllabled Mantra is as follows : "Klīm Kṛṣṇa Klīm"

The sage of this Mantra is Nārada, the metre is Gāyatrī and the deity is Kṛṣṇa.

The Ṣaḍaṅga Nyāsa has to be performed with Klīm is conjunction with the six long vowels.

Then the devotee should think of Hari as seated on the lotus growing from the root of Kalpa Vṛkṣa.

नौका: ध्यानमाह ।। पंचेति ।। निजसौन्द्रर्यमोहिताप्सरसम् ।।१००।।

नौका: ब्रह्मवृक्षजै: पलाशोत्थै ।।१०१-१०२।।

नौका: संक्रंदनादयइंद्रादय: ।।१०३।।

नौका: मंत्रांतर माह ।। कामेनेति ।। क्लींकृष्णक्लीमितिवेदाक्षरेश्चतुर्वर्ण: ।।१०४-१०५।।

Naukā: 100. *Dhyāna Verse.* He explains the Dhyāna. He has fascinated the divine damsels by means of his handsome features.

Naukā: 101-102. Brahmavṛksa - This is Palāśa tree.

Naukā: 103. Saṁkrandana and others - Indra and others.

Naukā: 104-105. He explains another Mantra "Klīm Kṛṣṇa Klīm"

Vedākṣara – having four syllables.

कल्पद्रोरतिरमणीयपल्लवेश्य:प्रोद्भूतैर्मणिनिकरै: प्रसिक्तमीशम् ।
ध्यायेयंकनकनिभांशुकेवसानंभुंजानंदधिनवनीतपायसानि ।।१०६।।

106. *Dhyāna Verse.* I shall meditate on the lord showered with heaps of gems coming out from the highly excellent sprouts of Kalpa tree. He is clad in two clothes resembling gold. He is in the act of eating curds, butter and milk pudding.

नौका: ध्यानमाह ।। कल्पेति ।। कल्पद्रो:कल्पवृक्षस्यप्रसिक्तमभिषिक्तम् ।।१०६।।

Naukā: 106. *Dhyāna Verse.* He explains Dhyāna

Kalpadroḥ – of the Kalpa tree

Prasikta - showered.

चतुर्लक्षजपेन्मंत्रं दशांशंबिल्वसंभवैः ।

फलैःप्रजुहुयादग्नौयजेदंगानिपूर्ववत् ॥१०७॥

महापद्मंतथापद्मंशखंमकरकच्छपौ ।

मुकुंदकुंदनीलाश्चनिधीन्दिक्षुसमर्चयेत् ॥१०८॥

इन्द्रादीन्वज्रपूर्वांश्चप्रयजेत्तदनंतरम् ।

इत्थंजपादि भिःसिद्धोमंत्रोनिधिरिवापरः ॥१०९॥

107-109. The devotee shall repeat the Mantra four hundred thousand times and perform fourty thousand Homas with the fruits of the Bilva tree. He shall adore the Aṇgas as before.

The Nidhis (treasure) Mahāpadma, Padma, Śaṅkha, Makara, Kacchapa, Mukunda, Kunda and Nīla shall be worshipped in the quarters.

Indra and others as well as thunderbolt and other weapons, also should be worshipped thereafter.

The Mantra that becomes perfectly realized thus by means of Japa etc. is like another treasure.

मत्रष्वेषुदशार्णोक्तान्प्रयोगान्विदधीतच ।

अथपुत्रप्रदंवच्मिकृष्णमत्रमनुष्टुभम् ॥११०॥

देवकीसुतवर्णांतेगोविंदपदमुच्चरेत् ।

वासुदेवपदंप्रोच्यसंबुद्ध्यंतंजगत्पतिम् ॥१११॥

देहिमेतनयंप्रोच्यकृष्ण त्वामहमीरयेत् ।

शरणंगतइत्युक्तोमंत्रोद्वात्रिंशदक्षरः ॥११२॥

110-112. In the case of all these Mantras the devotee can perform those rites for the realization of specific desires as mentioned in connection with the ten-syllabled Mantra.

Now I shall mention the 32 syllabled Mantra in the Anuṣṭup metre, that bestows sons. The Mantra is :

"Devakī Suta Govinda Vāsudeva Jagatpate Dehi Me Tanayam Kṛṣṇa Tvāmaham Śaraṇam Gataḥ".

नारदोमुनिरस्योक्तोनुष्टुप्छंदःसमीरितम् ।
देवः सुतप्रदःकृष्णःपादैःसर्वेणचांगकम् ॥११३॥

113. The sage of this Mantra is Nārada, the metre is Anuṣṭup, and the deity is Kṛṣṇa the bestower of sons. The five Aṅgas Nyāsas are to be performed with the feet severally and the whole Mantra collectively.

नौकाः मंत्रांतरमाह ॥ देवकीति ॥ यथा-देवकीसुतगोबिंदवासुदेवजगत्पते ॥ देहिमेतनयंकृष्णत्वामहंशरणंगतइति ॥१११-११३॥

Naukā: 111-113. He explains another Mantra (in verse form):

Devakīsuta Govinda Vāsudeva Jagatpate !

Dehi me Tanayam Kṛṣṇa Tvāmaham Śaraṇam Gataḥ !!

विजयेनयुतोरथस्थितःप्रसमानीयसमुद्रमध्यतः ।
प्रद दत्तनयान्द्विजन्मनेस्मरणीयोवसुदेवनंदनः ॥११४॥

114. *Dhyāna Verse.* The son of Vasudeva is to be rememhered as handing over his sons to a brahmin after having brought them from the middle of the ocean, seated in a Chriot in the company of Vijaya (*i.e.* Arjuna).

नौकाः ध्यानमाह ॥ विजयेनेति ॥ अर्जुनेनयुतोंबुधिमध्वात्तनयानाप्रीय-द्विजायददत्ध्येयः ॥११४॥

Naukā: 114. *Dhyāna Verse.* He explains Dhyna. Vijayena=Accompained by Arjuna. He brought the sons of the brahmin from the middle of the ocean and handed over to the brahmin. The lord should be meditated thus.

लक्षजपोयुंतंहोमस्तिलैर्मधुरसंयुतैः ।
अर्चापूर्वा दिताचैवंमंत्रःपुत्रप्रदोनृणाम् ॥११५॥

115. The Mantra has to be repeated a hundred thousand times. The Homas are to be performed thousand times with gingelly seeds mixed with sugar. The procedure for worship as before. This Mantra is the bestower of sons to men.

नृसिंहोमाधवारूढोलोहितोनिगमादिमः ।
कृशानुभार्य्यापंचार्णोम नुर्विषहरःपरः ॥११६॥

116. The five syllabled Mantra that removes poison is as follows :

"Kṣipa Om Svāha".

अनंन्तपंक्तिपक्षींद्रामुनिश्छंदश्चदेवता ।
तारवह्निप्रियेबीजशक्तिमंत्रस्यकीर्तिते ॥११७॥

117. The sage of this Mantra is Ananta; the metre is Paṅkti and the lord of birds is deity. Praṇava is the Bīja and Svāhā is Śakti.

हरिप्रसं गात्तद्वाहनस्यगरुडस्यमंत्रमाह ॥ नृसिंहइति ॥ नृसिंहःक्षः माधवारूडःइयुतः क्षि॥ लोहितःप ॥ निगमादिमः ॐ ॥ कृशानुभार्यान्वाहा ॥११६-११७॥

Naukā: 116-117. In the context of hari he explains the Mantra of Garuḍa the lords of vehicle

Nṛsiṁha = Kṣa

Mādhavāruḍha = Having I Hence Kṣi

Lohita = Pa

Nigamādimā = Om

Kṛśanubhāry – Svāhā.

ज्वलज्वलमहामतिस्वाहाहृदयमीरितम् ।
गरडेतिपदस्यांतेचूडाननशुचिप्रिया ॥११८॥

शिरोमं त्रोगरुडतःशिखेस्वाहाशिखामनुः ।
गरुडार्णानुदित्वांतेप्रभंजययुगंवेदेत् ॥११९॥
प्रभेदययुगंपश्चाद्वि त्रासयविमर्दय ।
प्रत्येकंद्विस्ततःस्वाहाकवचोमनुरीरितः ॥१२०॥
उग्ररूपधरांतेतुसर्वविषहरेतिच ।
भीषयद्वितयंप्रोच्यसर्वंदहदहेतिच ॥१२१॥
भस्मीकुरुकुरुस्वाहानेत्रमंत्रोयमीरितः ।
अप्रतिहतवर्णांते बलाप्रतिहतेतिच ॥१२२॥
शासनांतेतथाहुंफट्स्वाहास्त्रमनुरीरितः ।
पादेकटौहृदिमुखेमूर्ध्निवर्णान्प्रवि न्यसेत् ॥१२३॥

118-123. The requisite Mantras for the Ṣaḍaṅga Nyāsa are as follows :

"Jvala Jvala Mahāmati Svāhā" obeisance to the heart

"Garuḍa Cūḍānana Svāhā" Svāhā unto the head

"Garuḍa Śkhe Svāhā" Vaṣat unto the tuft

"Garuḍa Prabhañjaya Prabhañjaya, Vitrāsaya Vitrāsaya. Vimardaya Vimardaya Svāha" Hum unto the armour.

"Ugrarūpadhara Viṣahara Bhīsaya Bhīṣaya Sarvaṁ Daha Daha Bhasmī Kuru Kuru Svāhā" Vauṣaṭ unto the three eyes.

"Apratihatā Pratihata Śāsana Hum Phaṭ Svāha" Phaṭ unto the Astra.

The Nyāsas of the syllables are on the foot, hips, heart, mouth and the head.

नौकाः षडंगमाह ॥ ज्वलेति ॥ ज्वल २ महामतिस्वाहाहृत ॥ गरुडचूडाननन्वाहाशिरः ॥११८॥

नौकाः गरुडशिखेस्वाहाशिखा ॥ गरुडप्रभंजय २ प्रभेदय २ वित्रासय २ विमदर्य २ स्वाहाहुं ॥११९-१२०॥

नौका: उग्ररूपधरसर्वविषहरभीषय २ सर्वंदहदह भस्मीकुरुकुरुस्वाहा नेत्रम् ।। अप्रतिहतबलाप्रतिहतशासनहुंफट्स्वाहाअस्त्रम् ।। वर्णन्यासमाह ।। पादइति ।।१२१-१२३।।

Naukā: 118. He explains Ṣaḍaṅga Nyāsa

Jvala Jvala Mahā Mati Svāhā—heart

Garuḍa Cūḍānana Svāhā—head.

Naukā: 119-120. Garuḍa Śikhe Svāhā—Tuft

Garuḍa Prabhañjaya Prabhañjaya Prabhedaya Prabhedaya Vitrāsaya Vitrāsaya Vimardaya Vimardaya Svāhā—Hum.

Naukā: 121-123. Ugrarūpadhara Sarvaviṣahara Bhīṣaya Bhīṣ aya Sarvam Daha Daha Bhasmī Kuru Kuru Svāhā—the three eyes. Apratihata Balāpratihata Śāsana Hum Phaṭ Svāhā—Astram

He explains Varṇa Nyāsa—Pāda.

तप्तस्वर्णनिभंफणींद्रनिकरैःक्लृप्तांगभूषंप्रभुंस्मर्तॄणांशमयंतमुग्रम-खिलंनॄणांविषंतत्क्ष णात् ।

चंच्वग्रप्रचलद्भुजंगमभयंपाण्योर्वरंबिभ्रतंपक्षोच्चारितसामगीतममलं-श्रीपक्षिराजंभजे ।।१२४।।

124. *Dhyāna Verse.* I resort to the spottess holy king of the birds who resembles molten gold in colour, who has made the group of serpents his ornaments, who subdues instantaneously all the terrible poisons of the men who remember him in whose back lies a serpent shaking (with fear) who holds Vara gesture in his right hand and fearlessness in his left and who utters the Sāman songs by means of his wings.

नौका: ध्यानमाह ।। तप्तेति ।। स्मृर्तॄणांनृणामुग्रंविषंतत्क्षणाच्छमयति ।। दक्षेवरम्।। पक्षाभ्यामुच्चारिता:साम्नांबृहद्रथंतरादीनांगीतयोयेनतम् ।। बृहद्रथंतरे पक्षाविितिश्रुतेः ।।१२४।।

Naukā: 124. Dhyāna Verse. He explains Dhyāna. He suppresses instantaneosuly the poison of all the men who remember.

Vara in the right hand. By means of his wings he utters the songs of Bṛhadrathantara and other Sāmans. Because in the Veda it is mentioned that the Bṛhadrathantaras are his wings.।

पंचलक्षंजपेन्मंत्रंशांशंजुहुयात्तिलः ।
पूजयेन्मातृकापद्मेगरुडंवेदविग्रहम् ॥१२५॥
चतुर्थ्यंतःपक्षि राजःस्वाहापीठमनुःस्मृतः ।
इष्ट्वांगंकर्णिकामध्येनागान्पत्रेषुपूजयेत् ॥१२६॥
अनंतेवासुकिंचापितृ तीयंतक्षकंपुनः ।
कर्कोटकंतथापद्मंमहापद्मंसमर्चयेत् ॥१२७॥
शंखपालंचकुलिकमिंद्रादीन्वज्रसंयुतान् ।
एवंसिद्धेमनौमंत्रीनाशयेद्ग रलद्वयम् ॥१२८॥

125-128. The devotee shall repeat the Mantra five hundred thousand times and perform fifty thousand Homas with gingelly seeds. He shall worship in the Mātṛkā Padma, Garuḍa of the vedic form.

In the middle of the pericarp he worships the Aṅgas and the serpents in the petals. They are Ananta, Vāsuki, Takṣaka, Karkoṭaka, Padma, Mahāpadma, Śaṅkhapāla and Kulika.

Then he shall worship Indra and others along with their weapons thunderbolt etc.

When the Mantra is perfectly realized thus the devotee will be able to destroy the two types of poisons originating from the mobile beings as well as immobile beings.

विष्णुभक्तिपरोनित्यंयोभजेत्पक्षिनायकम् ।
शत्रून्सर्वा न्पराभूयसुखीभोगसमन्वितः ॥१२९॥
जीवेदनेकवर्षाणिसेवितोधरणीधवैः।
कलैवरांतेश्रीनाथसा युज्यंलभतेतुसः ॥१३०॥

129-130. The devotee with great reverence for Viṣṇu shall worship the lord of the birds constantly. He shall defeat all enemies and be happy with all sorts of enjoyments. Served even by kings he will live for many years. At the extinction of the body he will attain merging with Śrī Nātha (Lord Viṣṇu).

इतिमंत्रमहोदधौविष्णुगरुडमंत्रनिरूपणंनामचतुर्दशस्तरंगः ॥१४॥

नौकाः पक्षिराजायस्वाहेत्रिपीठमंत्रः ॥१२६-१२७॥

नौकाः गरलद्वयंविषद्वयंस्थावरजंगमाख्यम् ॥१२८-१२९॥

नौकाः धरणीधवैर्भूप तिभि:सेवितश्चिरंजीवित्वात्तनुक्षयेहरिसायुज्यंप्राप्नोति ॥१३०॥

Naukā: 126-127. The Mantra of the pedestal is –

"Pakṣirājāya Svāhā".

Naukā: 128-129. Garaladvayam the two kinds of poison - viz. that which arises from mobile being and immobile beings.

Naukā: 130. Dharaṇīdhavaiḥ – By kings. He will be served by them because of his longevity. On death he will attain merging with Hari.

इति श्रीमंत्रमहोदधिव्याख्यायांनौकायांविष्णुमंत्रकीर्तनंनामचतु
र्दशस्तरङ्गः ॥१४॥

Notes

6. According to the procedure followed by all Tantra treatises the worship starts immediately after the daily routine is over Vaiṣ ṇava devotees add a couple of rites more such as-Ācamana (ritualistic rinsing of the mouth) Prāṇāyāma and Nyāsa.

Pīṭha Pūjā. Om and Namaḥ for every deity such as Ādhāra Śakti, Prakṛti, Kūrma, Śeṣa, Ananta, Pṛthivī, Kṣīrasāgara, Śveta-dvīpa, Maṇimaṇḍapa, Kalpavṛkṣa, Maṇivedikā and Ratna. Simhāsana.

Thereafter Dharma etc. as well as Adharma etc. are worshipped.

In the middle of the pedestal Ananta and other deities, as. before, are worshipped.

The 32 aspects of Nṛsimha in the 32 petals are to be worshipped (Verse 9 et sq). One thing to be particularly noted here is that these aspects put emphasis on the terrible features and not the amiable ones.

51-52. Gopāla Mantra is a special feature in the Vaisnava process of worship.

According to Bṛhadgautamīya Tantra this Mantra is considered to be the bestower of both worldly enjoyment as well as ultimate salvation. The said text insists on adding the Kāma Bīja (*i.e.* Klīm) along with the Mantra for quick efficacy. Of course this initial augmentation is to be confuried to Japa, Pūjā and Homa. In the case of the additional rites cleansing of impurities and accretions, the inevitable results of the long tradition of oral transmission the Mantra is restricted to the original form of ten syllables. These rites are dealt with by the author in XXIV Taraṅga.

Keśava Kīrtyādi Nyāsa. This Nyāsa has been mentioned in

detail in the Gautamīya Tantra.

This is similar to Vighneśa Mātṛkā Nyāsa [XI-48 et sq] with, difference in deities which we give below: –

Keśava – Kīrti

Nārāyaṇa – Kānti

Mādhava – Tuṣṭi

Govinda – Puṣṭi

Visṇu-Dhṛti

Madhusūdana – Śānti

Trivikram – Kriyā

Vāmana – Dayā

Śrīdhara – Medhā

Hṛsīkeśa – Harṣā

Padmanābha – Śraddhā

Dāmodara – Lajjā

Vāsudeva -Lakṣmī

Saṁkarṣaṇa – Sarasvatī

Pradyumha – Prīti

Aniruddha – Rati

Cakrin – Jayā

Gadin – Durgā

Śārṅgin – Prabhā

Khaḍgin – Satyā

Śaṅkhin – Caṇḍā

Halin-Vāṇī

Musalin – Vilāsinī

Śūlin – Vijayā

Pāśin – Virajā

Aṅkuśin – Viśvā

Mukunda – Vinadā

Nandaja – Sunandā

Nandin – Smṛti

Nara-Ṛddhi

Narakajit – Samṛddhi

Hari – Śuddhi

Kṛṣṇa – Buddi

Satya – Bhakti

Sāttvata – Mati

Śauri – Kṣamā

Śūra – Ramā

Janārdana – Umā

Bhūdhara-Kledinī

Viśvamūrti – Klinnā

Vaikuṇṭha – Vasudā

Puruṣottama – Vasudhā

Balin – Parā

Balānuja – Parāyaṇa

Bāla – Sūkṣmā

Vṛṣaghna-Sandyā

Vṛṣa – Prajñā

Hamsa – Prabhā

Varāha – Niśā

Vimala – Amoghā

Nṛsimha – Vidyutā

Daśatattva Nyāsa, Vibhūti Pañjara Nyāsa are being dealt with later.